W9-AHZ-795

The Law School Admission Council (LSAC) is a nonprofit corporation that provides unique, state-of-the-art admission products and services to ease the admission process for law schools and their applicants worldwide. Currently, 221 law schools in the United States, Canada, and Australia are members of the Council and benefit from LSAC's services.

Print number
10 9 8 7 6 5 4 3 2 1

TABLE OF CONTENTS

INTRODUCTION TO THE LSAT

The Law School Admission Test is a half-day standardized test required for admission to all ABA-approved law schools, most Canadian law schools, and many other law schools. It consists of five 35-minute sections of multiple-choice questions. Four of the five sections contribute to the test taker's score. These sections include one Reading Comprehension section, one Analytical Reasoning section, and two Logical Reasoning sections. The unscored section, commonly referred to as the variable section, typically is used to pretest new test questions or to preequate new test forms. The placement of this section in the LSAT will vary. A 35-minute writing sample is administered at the end of the test. The writing sample is not scored by LSAC, but copies are sent to all law schools to which you apply. The score scale for the LSAT is 120 to 180.

The LSAT is designed to measure skills considered essential for success in law school: the reading and comprehension of complex texts with accuracy and insight; the organization and management of information and the ability to draw reasonable inferences from it; the ability to think critically; and the analysis and evaluation of the reasoning and arguments of others.

The LSAT provides a standard measure of acquired reading and verbal reasoning skills that law schools can use as one of several factors in assessing applicants.

For up-to-date information about LSAC's services, go to our website, LSAC.org.

SCORING

Your LSAT score is based on the number of questions you answer correctly (the raw score). There is no deduction for incorrect answers, and all questions count equally. In other words, there is no penalty for guessing.

Test Score Accuracy—Reliability and Standard Error of Measurement

Candidates perform at different levels on different occasions for reasons quite unrelated to the characteristics of a test itself. The accuracy of test scores is best described by the use of two related statistical terms: reliability and standard error of measurement.

Reliability is a measure of how consistently a test measures the skills being assessed. The higher the reliability coefficient for a test, the more certain we can be that test takers would get very similar scores if they took the test again.

LSAC reports an internal consistency measure of reliability for every test form. Reliability can vary from 0.00 to 1.00, and a test with no measurement error would have a reliability coefficient of 1.00 (never attained in practice). Reliability coefficients for past LSAT forms have ranged from .90 to .95, indicating a high degree of consistency for these tests. LSAC expects the reliability of the LSAT to continue to fall within the same range.

LSAC also reports the amount of measurement error associated with each test form, a concept known as the standard error of measurement (SEM). The SEM, which is usually about 2.6 points, indicates how close a test taker's observed score is likely to be to his or her true score. True scores are theoretical scores that would be obtained from perfectly reliable tests with no measurement error—scores never known in practice.

Score bands, or ranges of scores that contain a test taker's true score a certain percentage of the time, can be derived using the SEM. LSAT score bands are constructed by adding and subtracting the (rounded) SEM to and from an actual LSAT score (e.g., the LSAT score, plus or minus 3 points). Scores near 120 or 180 have asymmetrical bands. Score bands constructed in this manner will contain an individual's true score approximately 68 percent of the time.

Measurement error also must be taken into account when comparing LSAT scores of two test takers. It is likely that small differences in scores are due to measurement error rather than to meaningful differences in ability. The standard error of score differences provides some guidance as to the importance of differences between two scores. The standard error of score differences is approximately 1.4 times larger than the standard error of measurement for the individual scores.

Thus, a test score should be regarded as a useful but approximate measure of a test taker's abilities as measured by the test, not as an exact determination of his or her abilities. LSAC encourages law schools to examine the range of scores within the interval that probably contains the test taker's true score (e.g., the test taker's score band) rather than solely interpret the reported score alone.

Adjustments for Variation in Test Difficulty

All test forms of the LSAT reported on the same score scale are designed to measure the same abilities, but one test form may be slightly easier or more difficult than another. The scores from different test forms are made comparable through a statistical procedure known as equating. As a result of equating, a given scaled score earned on different test forms reflects the same level of ability.

Research on the LSAT

Summaries of LSAT validity studies and other LSAT research can be found in member law school libraries and at LSAC.org.

To Inquire About Test Questions

If you find what you believe to be an error or ambiguity in a test question that affects your response to the question, contact LSAC by e-mail: LSATTS@LSAC.org, or write to Law School Admission Council, Test Development Group, PO Box 40, Newtown, PA 18940-0040.

HOW THIS PREPTEST DIFFERS FROM AN ACTUAL LSAT

This PrepTest is made up of the scored sections and writing sample from the actual disclosed LSAT administered in November 2018. However, it does not contain the extra, variable section that is used to pretest new test items of one of the three multiple-choice question types. The three multiple-choice question types may be in a different order in an actual LSAT than in this PrepTest. This is because the order of these question types is intentionally varied for each administration of the test.

THE THREE LSAT MULTIPLE-CHOICE QUESTION TYPES

The multiple-choice questions that make up most of the LSAT reflect a broad range of academic disciplines and are intended to give no advantage to candidates from a particular academic background.

The five sections of the test contain three different question types. The following material presents a general discussion of the nature of each question type and some strategies that can be used in answering them.

Analytical Reasoning Questions

Analytical Reasoning questions are designed to assess the ability to consider a group of facts and rules, and, given those facts and rules, determine what could or must be true. The specific scenarios associated with these questions are usually unrelated to law, since they are intended to be accessible to a wide range of test takers. However, the skills tested parallel those involved in determining what could or must be the case given a set of regulations, the terms of a contract, or the facts of a legal case in relation to the law. In Analytical Reasoning questions, you are asked to reason deductively from a set of statements and rules or principles that describe relationships among persons, things, or events.

Analytical Reasoning questions appear in sets, with each set based on a single passage. The passage used for each set of questions describes common ordering relationships or grouping relationships, or a combination of both types of relationships. Examples include scheduling employees for work shifts, assigning instructors to class sections, ordering tasks according to priority, and distributing grants for projects.

Analytical Reasoning questions test a range of deductive reasoning skills. These include:

- Comprehending the basic structure of a set of relationships by determining a complete solution to the problem posed (for example, an acceptable seating arrangement of all six diplomats around a table)

- Reasoning with conditional ("if-then") statements and recognizing logically equivalent formulations of such statements

- Inferring what could be true or must be true from given facts and rules

- Inferring what could be true or must be true from given facts and rules together with new information in the form of an additional or substitute fact or rule

- Recognizing when two statements are logically equivalent in context by identifying a condition or rule that could replace one of the original conditions while still resulting in the same possible outcomes

Analytical Reasoning questions reflect the kinds of detailed analyses of relationships and sets of constraints that a law student must perform in legal problem solving. For example, an Analytical Reasoning passage might describe six diplomats being seated around a table, following certain rules of protocol as to who can sit where. You, the test taker, must answer questions about the logical implications of given and new information. For example, you may be asked who can sit between diplomats X and Y, or who cannot sit next to X if W sits next to Y. Similarly, if you were a student in law school, you might be asked to analyze a scenario involving a set of particular circumstances and a set of governing rules in the form of constitutional provisions, statutes, administrative codes, or prior rulings that have been upheld. You might then be asked to determine the legal options in the scenario: what is required given the scenario, what is permissible given the scenario, and what is prohibited given the scenario. Or you might be asked to develop a "theory" for the case: when faced with an incomplete set of facts about the case, you must fill in the picture based on what is implied by the facts that are known. The problem could be elaborated by the addition of new information or hypotheticals.

No formal training in logic is required to answer these questions correctly. Analytical Reasoning questions are intended to be answered using knowledge, skills, and reasoning ability generally expected of college students and graduates.

Suggested Approach

Some people may prefer to answer first those questions about a passage that seem less difficult and then those that seem more difficult. In general, it is best to finish one passage before starting on another, because much time can be lost in returning to a passage and reestablishing familiarity with its relationships. However, if you are having great difficulty on one particular set of questions and are spending too much time on them, it may be to your advantage to skip that set of questions and go on to the next passage, returning to the problematic set of questions after you have finished the other questions in the section.

Do not assume that because the conditions for a set of questions look long or complicated, the questions based on those conditions will be especially difficult.

Read the passage carefully. Careful reading and analysis are necessary to determine the exact nature of the relationships involved in an Analytical Reasoning passage. Some relationships are fixed (for example, P and R must always work on the same project). Other relationships are variable (for example, Q must be assigned to either team 1 or team 3). Some relationships that are not stated explicitly in the conditions are implied by and can be deduced from those that are stated (for example, if one condition about paintings in a display specifies that Painting K must be to the left of Painting Y, and another specifies that Painting W must be to the left of Painting K, then it can be deduced that Painting W must be to the left of Painting Y).

In reading the conditions, do not introduce unwarranted assumptions. For instance, in a set of questions establishing relationships of height and weight among the members of a team, do not assume that a person who is taller than another person must weigh more than that person. As another example, suppose a set involves ordering and a question in the set asks what must be true if both X and Y must be earlier than Z; in this case, do not assume that X must be earlier than Y merely because X is mentioned before Y. All the information needed to answer each question is provided in the passage and the question itself.

The conditions are designed to be as clear as possible. Do not interpret the conditions as if they were intended to trick you. For example, if a question asks how many people could be eligible to serve on a committee, consider only those people named in the passage unless directed otherwise. When in doubt, read the conditions in their most obvious sense. Remember, however, that the language in the conditions is intended to be read for precise meaning. It is essential to pay particular attention to words that describe or limit relationships, such as "only," "exactly," "never," "always," "must be," "cannot be," and the like.

The result of this careful reading will be a clear picture of the structure of the relationships involved, including the kinds of relationships permitted, the participants in the relationships, and the range of possible actions or attributes for these participants.

Keep in mind question independence. Each question should be considered separately from the other questions in its set. No information, except what is given in the original conditions, should be carried over from one question to another.

In some cases a question will simply ask for conclusions to be drawn from the conditions as originally given. Some questions may, however, add information to the original conditions or temporarily suspend or replace one of the original conditions for the purpose of that question only. For example, if Question 1 adds the supposition "if P is sitting at table 2 ...," this supposition should NOT be carried over to any other question in the set.

Consider highlighting text and using diagrams. Many people find it useful to underline key points in the passage and in each question. In addition, it may prove very helpful to draw a diagram to assist you in finding the solution to the problem.

In preparing for the test, you may wish to experiment with different types of diagrams. For a scheduling problem, a simple calendar-like diagram may be helpful. For a grouping problem, an array of labeled columns or rows may be useful.

Even though most people find diagrams to be very helpful, some people seldom use them, and for some individual questions no one will need a diagram. There is by no means universal agreement on which kind of diagram is best for which problem or in which cases a diagram is most useful. Do not be concerned if a particular problem in the test seems to be best approached without the use of a diagram.

Logical Reasoning Questions

Arguments are a fundamental part of the law, and analyzing arguments is a key element of legal analysis. Training in the law builds on a foundation of basic reasoning skills. Law students must draw on the skills of analyzing, evaluating, constructing, and refuting arguments. They need to be able to identify what information is relevant to an issue or argument and what impact further evidence might have. They need to be able to reconcile opposing positions and use arguments to persuade others.

Logical Reasoning questions evaluate the ability to analyze, critically evaluate, and complete arguments as they occur in ordinary language. The questions are based on short arguments drawn from a wide variety of sources, including newspapers, general interest magazines, scholarly publications, advertisements, and informal discourse. These arguments mirror legal reasoning in the types of arguments presented and in their complexity, though few of the arguments actually have law as a subject matter.

Each Logical Reasoning question requires you to read and comprehend a short passage, then answer one question (or, rarely, two questions) about it. The questions are designed to assess a wide range of skills involved in thinking critically, with an emphasis on skills that are central to legal reasoning.

These skills include:

• Recognizing the parts of an argument and their relationships

• Recognizing similarities and differences between patterns of reasoning

• Drawing well-supported conclusions

• Reasoning by analogy

• Recognizing misunderstandings or points of disagreement

• Determining how additional evidence affects an argument

• Detecting assumptions made by particular arguments

• Identifying and applying principles or rules

• Identifying flaws in arguments

• Identifying explanations

The questions do not presuppose specialized knowledge of logical terminology. For example, you will not be expected to know the meaning of specialized terms such as "ad hominem" or "syllogism." On the other hand, you will be expected to understand and critique the reasoning contained in arguments. This requires that you possess a university-level understanding of widely used concepts such as argument, premise, assumption, and conclusion.

Suggested Approach

Read each question carefully. Make sure that you understand the meaning of each part of the question. Make sure that you understand the meaning of each answer choice and the ways in which it may or may not relate to the question posed.

Do not pick a response simply because it is a true statement. Although true, it may not answer the question posed.

Answer each question on the basis of the information that is given, even if you do not agree with it. Work within the context provided by the passage. LSAT questions do not involve any tricks or hidden meanings.

Reading Comprehension Questions

Both law school and the practice of law revolve around extensive reading of highly varied, dense, argumentative, and expository texts (for example, cases, codes, contracts, briefs, decisions, evidence). This reading must be exacting, distinguishing precisely what is said from what is not said. It involves comparison, analysis, synthesis, and application (for example, of principles and rules). It involves drawing appropriate inferences and applying ideas and arguments to new contexts. Law school reading also requires the ability to grasp unfamiliar subject matter and the ability to penetrate difficult and challenging material.

The purpose of LSAT Reading Comprehension questions is to measure the ability to read, with understanding and insight, examples of lengthy and complex materials similar to those commonly encountered in law school. The Reading Comprehension section of the LSAT contains four sets of reading questions, each set consisting of a selection of reading material followed by five to eight questions. The reading selection in three of the four sets consists of a single reading passage; the other set contains two related shorter passages. Sets with two passages are a variant of Reading Comprehension called Comparative Reading, which was introduced in June 2007.

Comparative Reading questions concern the relationships between the two passages, such as those of generalization/instance, principle/application, or point/counterpoint. Law school work often requires reading two or more texts in conjunction with each other and understanding their relationships. For example, a law student may read a trial court decision together with an appellate court decision that overturns it, or identify the fact pattern from a hypothetical suit together with the potentially controlling case law.

Reading selections for LSAT Reading Comprehension questions are drawn from a wide range of subjects in the humanities, the social sciences, the biological and physical sciences, and areas related to the law. Generally, the selections are densely written, use high-level vocabulary, and contain sophisticated argument or complex rhetorical structure (for example, multiple points of view). Reading Comprehension questions require you to read carefully and accurately, to determine the relationships among the various parts of the reading selection, and to draw reasonable inferences from the material in the selection. The questions may ask about the following characteristics of a passage or pair of passages:

• The main idea or primary purpose

• Information that is explicitly stated

• Information or ideas that can be inferred

- The meaning or purpose of words or phrases as used in context

- The organization or structure

- The application of information in the selection to a new context

- Principles that function in the selection

- Analogies to claims or arguments in the selection

- An author's attitude as revealed in the tone of a passage or the language used

- The impact of new information on claims or arguments in the selection

Suggested Approach

Since reading selections are drawn from many different disciplines and sources, you should not be discouraged if you encounter material with which you are not familiar. It is important to remember that questions are to be answered exclusively on the basis of the information provided in the selection. There is no particular knowledge that you are expected to bring to the test, and you should not make inferences based on any prior knowledge of a subject that you may have. You may, however, wish to defer working on a set of questions that seems particularly difficult or unfamiliar until after you have dealt with sets you find easier.

Strategies. One question that often arises in connection with Reading Comprehension has to do with the most effective and efficient order in which to read the selections and questions. Possible approaches include:

- reading the selection very closely and then answering the questions;

- reading the questions first, reading the selection closely, and then returning to the questions; or

- skimming the selection and questions very quickly, then rereading the selection closely and answering the questions.

Test takers are different, and the best strategy for one might not be the best strategy for another. In preparing for the test, therefore, you might want to experiment with the different strategies and decide what works most effectively for you.

Remember that your strategy must be effective under timed conditions. For this reason, the first strategy—reading the selection very closely and then answering the questions—may be the most effective for you. Nonetheless, if you believe that one of the other strategies

might be more effective for you, you should try it out and assess your performance using it.

Reading the selection. Whatever strategy you choose, you should give the passage or pair of passages at least one careful reading before answering the questions. Try to distinguish main ideas from supporting ideas, and opinions or attitudes from factual, objective information. Note transitions from one idea to the next and identify the relationships among the different ideas or parts of a passage, or between the two passages in Comparative Reading sets. Consider how and why an author makes points and draws conclusions. Be sensitive to implications of what the passages say.

You may find it helpful to mark key parts of passages. For example, you might underline main ideas or important arguments, and you might circle transitional words—"although," "nevertheless," "correspondingly," and the like—that will help you map the structure of a passage. Also, you might note descriptive words that will help you identify an author's attitude toward a particular idea or person.

Answering the Questions

- Always read all the answer choices before selecting the best answer. The best answer choice is the one that most accurately and completely answers the question being posed.

- Respond to the specific question being asked. Do not pick an answer choice simply because it is a true statement. For example, picking a true statement might yield an incorrect answer to a question in which you are asked to identify an author's position on an issue, since you are not being asked to evaluate the truth of the author's position but only to correctly identify what that position is.

- Answer the questions only on the basis of the information provided in the selection. Your own views, interpretations, or opinions, and those you have heard from others, may sometimes conflict with those expressed in a reading selection; however, you are expected to work within the context provided by the reading selection. You should not expect to agree with everything you encounter in Reading Comprehension passages.

THE WRITING SAMPLE

On the day of the test, you will be asked to write one sample essay. LSAC does not score the writing sample, but copies are sent to all law schools to which you apply. According to a 2015 LSAC survey of 129 United States and Canadian law schools, almost all utilize the writing sample in evaluating some applications for admission. Failure to respond to writing sample prompts and frivolous responses have been used by law schools as grounds for rejection of applications for admission.

In developing and implementing the writing sample portion of the LSAT, LSAC has operated on the following premises: First, law schools and the legal profession value highly the ability to communicate effectively in writing. Second, it is important to encourage potential law students to develop effective writing skills. Third, a sample of an applicant's writing, produced under controlled conditions, is a potentially useful indication of that person's writing ability. Fourth, the writing sample can serve as an independent check on other writing submitted by applicants as part of the admission process. Finally, writing samples may be useful for diagnostic purposes related to improving a candidate's writing.

The writing prompt presents a decision problem. You are asked to make a choice between two positions or courses of action. Both of the choices are defensible, and you are given criteria and facts on which to base your decision. There is no "right" or "wrong" position to take on the topic, so the quality of each test taker's response is a function not of which choice is made, but of how well or poorly the choice is supported and how well or poorly the other choice is criticized.

The LSAT writing prompt was designed and validated by legal education professionals. Since it involves writing based on fact sets and criteria, the writing sample gives applicants the opportunity to demonstrate the type of argumentative writing that is required in law school, although the topics are usually nonlegal.

You will have 35 minutes in which to plan and write an essay on the topic you receive. Read the topic and the accompanying directions carefully. You will probably find it best to spend a few minutes considering the topic and organizing your thoughts before you begin writing. In your essay, be sure to develop your ideas fully, leaving time, if possible, to review what you have written. Do not write on a topic other than the one specified. Writing on a topic of your own choice is not acceptable.

No special knowledge is required or expected for this writing exercise. Law schools are interested in the reasoning, clarity, organization, language usage, and writing mechanics displayed in your essay. How well you write is more important than how much you write. Confine your essay to the blocked, lined area on the front and back of the separate Writing Sample Response Sheet. Only that area will be reproduced for law schools. Be sure that your writing is legible.

TAKING THE PREPTEST UNDER SIMULATED LSAT CONDITIONS

One important way to prepare for the LSAT is to simulate the day of the test by taking a practice test under actual time constraints. Taking a practice test under timed conditions helps you to estimate the amount of time you can afford to spend on each question in a section and to determine the question types on which you may need additional practice.

Since the LSAT is a timed test, it is important to use your allotted time wisely. During the test, you may work only on the section designated by the test supervisor. You cannot devote extra time to a difficult section and make up that time on a section you find easier. In pacing yourself, and checking your answers, you should think of each section of the test as a separate minitest.

Be sure that you answer every question on the test. When you do not know the correct answer to a question, first eliminate the responses that you know are incorrect, then make your best guess among the remaining choices. Do not be afraid to guess as there is no penalty for incorrect answers.

When you take a practice test, abide by all the requirements specified in the directions and keep strictly within the specified time limits. Work without a rest period. When you take an actual test, you will have only a short break—usually 10–15 minutes—after SECTION III.

When taken under conditions as much like actual testing conditions as possible, a practice test provides very useful preparation for taking the LSAT.

Official directions for the four multiple-choice sections and the writing sample are included in this PrepTest so that you can approximate actual testing conditions as you practice.

To take the test:

- Set a timer for 35 minutes. Answer all the questions in SECTION I of this PrepTest. Stop working on that section when the 35 minutes have elapsed.

- Repeat, allowing yourself 35 minutes each for sections II, III, and IV.

- Set the timer again for 35 minutes, then prepare your response to the writing sample topic at the end of this PrepTest.

- Refer to "Computing Your Score" for the PrepTest for instruction on evaluating your performance. An answer key is provided for that purpose.

The practice test that follows consists of four sections corresponding to the four scored sections of the November 2018 LSAT. Also reprinted is the November 2018 unscored writing sample topic.

General Directions for the LSAT Answer Sheet

This portion of the test consists of five multiple-choice sections, each with a time limit of 35 minutes. The supervisor will tell you when to begin and end each section. If you finish a section before time is called, you may check your work on that section **only**; do not turn to any other section of the test book and do not work on any other section either in the test book or on the answer sheet.

There are several different types of questions on the test, and each question type has its own directions. **Be sure you understand the directions for each question type before attempting to answer any questions in that section.**

Not everyone will finish all the questions in the time allowed. Do not hurry, but work steadily and as quickly as you can without sacrificing accuracy. You are advised to use your time effectively. If a question seems too difficult, go on to the next one and return to the difficult question after completing the section. **MARK THE BEST ANSWER YOU CAN FOR EVERY QUESTION. NO DEDUCTIONS WILL BE MADE FOR WRONG ANSWERS. YOUR SCORE WILL BE BASED ONLY ON THE NUMBER OF QUESTIONS YOU ANSWER CORRECTLY.**

ALL YOUR ANSWERS MUST BE MARKED ON THE ANSWER SHEET. Answer spaces for each question are lettered to correspond with the letters of the potential answers to each question in the test book. After you have decided which of the answers is correct, blacken the corresponding space on the answer sheet. **BE SURE THAT EACH MARK IS BLACK AND COMPLETELY FILLS THE ANSWER SPACE.** Give only one answer to each question. If you change an answer, be sure that all previous marks are **erased completely.** Since the answer sheet is machine scored, incomplete erasures may be interpreted as intended answers. **ANSWERS RECORDED IN THE TEST BOOK WILL NOT BE SCORED.**

There may be more question numbers on this answer sheet than there are questions in a section. Do not be concerned, but be certain that the section and number of the question you are answering matches the answer sheet section and question number. Additional answer spaces in any answer sheet section should be left blank. Begin your next section in the number one answer space for that section.

LSAC takes various steps to ensure that answer sheets are returned from test centers in a timely manner for processing. In the unlikely event that an answer sheet is not received, LSAC will permit the examinee either to retest at no additional fee or to receive a refund of his or her LSAT fee. **THESE REMEDIES ARE THE ONLY REMEDIES AVAILABLE IN THE UNLIKELY EVENT THAT AN ANSWER SHEET IS NOT RECEIVED BY LSAC.**

HOW DID YOU PREPARE FOR THE LSAT?
(Select all that apply.)

Responses to this item are voluntary and will be used for statistical research purposes only.

○ By using Khan Academy's official LSAT practice material.
○ By taking the free sample questions and/or free sample LSAT available on LSAC's website.
○ By working through official LSAT *PrepTest* and/or other LSAC test prep products.
○ By using LSAT prep books or software **not** published by LSAC.
○ By attending a commercial test preparation or coaching course.
○ By attending a test preparation or coaching course offered through an undergraduate institution.
○ Self study.
○ Other preparation.
○ No preparation.

CERTIFYING STATEMENT

Please write the following statement. Sign and date.

I certify that I am the examinee whose name appears on this answer sheet and that I am here to take the LSAT for the sole purpose of being considered for admission to law school. I further certify that I will neither assist nor receive assistance from any other candidate, and I agree not to copy, retain, or transmit examination questions in any form or discuss them with any other person.

_____

_____

_____

_____

_____

_____

SIGNATURE: _____   TODAY'S DATE: _____ / _____ / _____
                                                MONTH   DAY   YEAR

DO NOT WRITE IN THIS BOX.

FOR LSAC USE ONLY   ⬤

Law School Admission Council

INSTRUCTIONS FOR COMPLETING THE BIOGRAPHICAL AREA ARE ON THE BACK COVER OF YOUR TEST BOOKLET.
USE ONLY A NO. 2 OR HB PENCIL TO COMPLETE THIS ANSWER SHEET. DO NOT USE INK.

A

1 LAST NAME | **FIRST NAME** | **MI**

2 LAST 4 DIGITS OF SOCIAL SECURITY/ SOCIAL INSURANCE NO.

L

3 LSAC ACCOUNT NUMBER

4 CENTER NUMBER

5 DATE OF BIRTH

MONTH	DAY	YEAR
Jan		
Feb		
Mar		
Apr		
May		
June		
July		
Aug		
Sept		
Oct		
Nov		
Dec		

6 TEST FORM CODE

7 TEST DATE

MONTH / DAY / YEAR

8 TEST FORM

9 TEST BOOK SERIAL NO.

Law School Admission Test

Mark one and only one answer to each question. Be sure to fill in completely the space for your intended answer choice. If you erase, do so completely. Make no stray marks.

SECTION 1 | **SECTION 2** | **SECTION 3** | **SECTION 4** | **SECTION 5**

Questions 1–30 for each section, answer choices A B C D E

10 PLEASE PRINT INFORMATION

LAST NAME

FIRST NAME

DATE OF BIRTH

Law School Admission Council

THE PREPTEST

1

SECTION I
Time—35 minutes
25 Questions

Directions: Each question in this section is based on the reasoning presented in a brief passage. In answering the questions, you should not make assumptions that are by commonsense standards implausible, superfluous, or incompatible with the passage. For some questions, more than one of the choices could conceivably answer the question. However, you are to choose the best answer; that is, choose the response that most accurately and completely answers the question and mark that response on your answer sheet.

1. Researcher: During the rainy season, bonobos (an ape species closely related to chimpanzees) frequently swallow whole the rough-surfaced leaves of the shrub *Manniophyton fulvum*. These leaves are likely ingested because of their medicinal properties, since ingestion of these leaves facilitates the elimination of gastrointestinal worms.

Which one of the following, if true, most strengthens the researcher's argument?

(A) Bonobos rarely swallow whole leaves of any plants other than *M. fulvum*.

(B) Chimpanzees have also been observed to swallow rough-surfaced leaves whole during the rainy season.

(C) Of the rough-leaved plants available to bonobos, *M. fulvum* shrubs are the most common.

(D) The leaves of *M. fulvum* are easier to swallow whole when they are wet.

(E) The rainy season is the time when bonobos are most likely to be infected with gastrointestinal worms.

2. Policy analyst: Those concerned with safeguarding public health by reducing the risk of traffic fatalities typically focus their efforts on automotive safety measures such as increasing seat belt use, reducing distracted driving, and improving automotive technology. But what would contribute the most to safeguarding public health is a reduction in total miles traveled on our roads. The fact is that traveling by car is itself a major risk factor.

Which one of the following most accurately expresses the overall conclusion drawn in the policy analyst's argument?

(A) Public health can be safeguarded through reducing traffic fatalities.

(B) Those concerned with safeguarding public health should focus their efforts on reducing traffic fatalities.

(C) Increasing seat belt use, reducing distracted driving, and improving automotive technology all safeguard public health.

(D) A reduction in total miles traveled would contribute more to safeguarding public health than would any automotive safety measure.

(E) Traveling by car is itself a major risk factor for traffic fatalities.

GO ON TO THE NEXT PAGE.

3. Letter to the Editor: The arts section of this paper shows a lamentable bias toward movies and against local theatrical productions. Over the last year alone, the paper has published over five times as many movie reviews as reviews of live plays.

Which one of the following, if true, most seriously weakens the argument?

(A) Some newspapers do not publish any reviews of live plays.

(B) The number of movies released last year was significantly greater than the number of live plays performed locally.

(C) The newspaper has five movie critics, but only one theater critic.

(D) The newspaper does not have the space in the arts section to publish a review of every movie that is released or every live play that is locally performed.

(E) The newspaper published more reviews of live plays in the last year than it did two years ago.

4. Archaeologist: Our university museum possesses several ancient artifacts whose ownership is in dispute. Although the museum has documentation showing that the items were obtained legally, there is an overriding principle that any important ancient artifact belongs by rights to the nation on whose territory it was discovered. Given that an institution is obliged to honor those rights, our museum should return the artifacts.

Which one of the following most accurately expresses the overall conclusion of the archaeologist's argument?

(A) The university museum should return the ancient artifacts in dispute.

(B) Any important ancient artifact belongs by rights to the nation on whose territory it was discovered.

(C) The ancient artifacts whose ownership is in dispute were obtained legally by the university museum.

(D) The university museum is in possession of several artifacts whose ownership is in dispute.

(E) There is an overriding principle that any important ancient artifact belongs by rights to the nation on whose territory it was discovered.

5. Many fictional works have characters who are supposedly precognitive—that is, able to accurately perceive future events. But a perception of a future event is accurate only if that event comes to pass. Thus, the plots of these works often show that the characters are not truly precognitive, since some of the future events the characters perceive do not in fact come to pass.

Which one of the following is an assumption on which the argument depends?

(A) A character is truly precognitive only if all of that character's perceptions of future events are accurate.

(B) It is impossible for someone to perceive future events accurately with absolute consistency.

(C) The plots of fictional works that portray characters as precognitive often do not specify whether the future events those characters perceive come to pass.

(D) When fictional works portray characters as precognitive, those characters' perceptions of future events are generally central to the plots of those works.

(E) No work of fiction has portrayed a truly precognitive character.

6. Economist: There have been large declines in employment around the globe, so it's not surprising that the number of workers injured on the job has decreased. What is surprising, however, is that the percentage of workers injured on the job has also decreased.

Each of the following, if true, helps to explain the surprising result mentioned by the economist EXCEPT:

(A) Overall, people who are employed are working fewer hours each day.

(B) A decrease in the demand for products has reduced the pressure on workers to meet production quotas and deadlines.

(C) Some of the most dangerous industries have had especially big declines in employment.

(D) There has been a general decline in the resources devoted to workplace safety.

(E) Inexperienced workers have lost their jobs at higher rates than experienced ones.

GO ON TO THE NEXT PAGE.

7. Editorial: Animated films appropriate for children are those that are innocently whimsical, mischievous perhaps, but not threatening. Since new animated films aimed at adults have dark themes such as poverty and despair, such films cannot be considered appropriate for children.

Which one of the following is an assumption that would allow the conclusion to be properly drawn?

(A) Films that are whimsical and mischievous are not threatening.

(B) Films that are appropriate for adults are seldom appropriate for children.

(C) Films that have dark themes are threatening.

(D) Children enjoy films only if the films include animation.

(E) Children do not attend to some details in films aimed at adults.

8. Monarch butterflies must contend with single-celled parasites that can cause deformities that interfere with their flight. In populations of monarch butterflies that have not migrated, as many as 95 percent are heavily infected by the parasites, while less than 15 percent of those in migrating populations are infected. This shows that migrating allows monarch butterflies to avoid these parasites.

The reasoning in the argument is flawed in that the argument overlooks the possibility that

(A) monarch butterflies are unable to detect which areas are free from parasites

(B) long migrations are no better protection from parasites than are short migrations

(C) populations of monarch butterflies that have not migrated are much larger than migrating populations

(D) monarch butterflies infected with parasites are typically unable to migrate

(E) populations of monarch butterflies tend not to migrate if they have stable food sources

9. Legal doctrine: The government cannot appropriate private property without offering fair compensation to the property owner.

Application: If the government institutes a regulation that blocks construction on undeveloped private lots on the shore of Lake Crowell—thereby diminishing their market value—it must offer fair compensation to the owners of that property.

Which one of the following principles, if valid, most justifies the above application of the legal doctrine?

(A) A government should not implement a regulation on lakeside property that it would not implement on other types of property.

(B) Governments must balance the rights of private property holders with the rights of those who value undeveloped wilderness environments.

(C) Regulations that significantly diminish the economic value of a piece of property constitute an appropriation of that property.

(D) Owners of private property are alone responsible for the economic risks associated with government regulations that affect the use of that property.

(E) A government can appropriate private property only if it is in response to a compelling public interest.

10. When a bird flies, powerful forces converge on its shoulder joints. The bird's wings must be kept stable during flight, which cannot happen unless something balances these forces. The only structure in birds capable of balancing them is a ligament that connects the wing to the shoulder joint. So that ligament must be _____.

Which one of the following most logically completes the argument?

(A) the only structure that is indispensable to bird flight

(B) the reason that a bird's wings must be kept stable during flight

(C) the sole connection between the wing and the shoulder joint

(D) the source of the powerful forces that converge on the shoulder joint

(E) the means by which a bird stabilizes its wings during flight

GO ON TO THE NEXT PAGE.

11. As part of a project to enhance the downtown area, the transit authority plans to build a majestic new subway station on the Longview line. However, the current design of the station does not include a connection to the nearby Waterfront line. Adding a tunnel from the station to the Waterfront line using the current design would make the station much more convenient to commuters but would also put the project over budget. Since the budget cannot be increased, a more modest station should be built so that a tunnel can be included.

Which one of the following principles, if valid, most helps to justify the reasoning in the argument above?

(A) The transit authority should design a subway station that costs less than the amount budgeted.

(B) The transit authority should consider all potential additions to the subway station that would make it more convenient to commuters.

(C) In the enhancement of the downtown area, convenience to commuters should be given priority over majestic design.

(D) Unless a subway station can be built within budget that is both convenient to commuters and in keeping with the new design, the transit authority should abandon plans to build a station.

(E) The new subway station should enhance the downtown area more than any other potential project that is similar in cost.

12. A study found that most of the strokes diagnosed by doctors occurred in the left side of patients' brains. This suggests that right-side strokes are more likely than left-side strokes to go undiagnosed since _____.

The conclusion of the argument is strongly supported if which one of the following completes the passage?

(A) patients who have strokes typically also have other health problems

(B) it is very likely that just as many strokes occur in the right side of the brain as in the left side

(C) doctors vary greatly in the accuracy of their diagnoses of strokes

(D) the symptoms of right-side strokes tend to be different than the symptoms of left-side strokes

(E) other studies have suggested that a large number of minor strokes go undiagnosed

13. When so many oysters died off the coast of Britain that some native species were threatened with extinction, the fact that the water temperature had recently risen was at first thought to be the cause. Later, however, the cause was determined to be the chemical tributyl tin (TBT), used to keep barnacles off the hulls of boats. Legislation that banned TBT has nearly eliminated that chemical from British waters, yet the populations of the endangered oyster species have not grown.

Which one of the following, if true, most helps to explain the failure of the native oyster populations to recover?

(A) The increase in water temperature has slowed in the years since the legislation was passed.

(B) Native oysters rely on different sources of food than do the barnacles that live on the hulls of boats.

(C) TBT also killed imported varieties of oysters that flourish at the expense of native oysters now that the waters are warmer.

(D) Other chemicals that are used to remove barnacles from the hulls of boats seem to have little effect on the oyster populations.

(E) TBT is more deadly to oysters in colder waters than in warmer waters.

14. Pratt: Almost all cases of rabies in humans come from being bitten by a rabid animal, and bats do carry rabies. But there is little justification for health warnings that urge the removal of any bats residing in buildings where people work or live. Bats are shy animals that rarely bite, and the overwhelming majority of bats do not have rabies.

Which one of the following, if true, most weakens Pratt's argument?

(A) A rabid bat is much more likely to infect another bat than to infect any other type of animal.

(B) Rabid bats are less mobile than other bats but are much more aggressive.

(C) Most animals that carry rabies are animals of species that, under normal conditions, very rarely bite people.

(D) The bat species with the highest incidence of rabies do not live in buildings.

(E) People are more likely to be aware of having been bitten by a bat if they were bitten by the bat inside a building.

GO ON TO THE NEXT PAGE.

15. It has been said that understanding a person completely leads one to forgive that person entirely. If so, then it follows that complete self-forgiveness is beyond our reach, for complete self-understanding, however desirable, is unattainable.

A flaw in the reasoning in the argument above is that this argument

(A) treats the failure to satisfy a condition that brings about a particular outcome as if satisfying that condition is the only way to realize the outcome

(B) confuses something that is necessary for an action to occur with something that necessarily results from that action

(C) takes for granted that something that has merely been said to be true is, in fact, true

(D) ignores the possibility that a state of affairs is desirable even if it cannot be attained

(E) uses the difficulty of attaining a state of affairs as a reason for not attempting to attain it

16. A popular complaint about abstract expressionist paintings—that "a child could paint that"—holds that their stylistic similarities to young children's paintings show that they are no more aesthetically pleasing than those inexpert works. But most participants in a psychological study, when shown pairs of paintings consisting of an abstract expressionist painting and a preschooler's painting, consistently rated the abstract expressionist painting as aesthetically better, refuting this complaint and thereby establishing that abstract expressionist paintings are aesthetically pleasing.

The argument depends on assuming which one of the following?

(A) People are better at judging the aesthetic value of a painting when they compare it with another painting.

(B) Most of the preschoolers' paintings used in the study were not aesthetically displeasing.

(C) Each painting shown to the participants had a label that accurately indicated whether it was an abstract expressionist painting or a preschooler's painting.

(D) Participants who did not consistently rate the abstract expressionist paintings as aesthetically better nonetheless rated them better more often than not.

(E) There were few stylistic similarities between the abstract expressionist paintings that participants were shown and the preschoolers' paintings with which they were paired.

17. Xavier: The new fast-food place on 10th Street is out of business already. I'm not surprised. It had no indoor seating, and few people want to sit outside and breathe exhaust fumes while they eat.

Miranda: The bank should have realized that with all the fast-food places on 10th Street, one lacking indoor seating was likely to fail. So it was irresponsible of them to lend the money for it.

It can be inferred from the dialogue that Xavier and Miranda agree that

(A) few people want to sit outside while they eat

(B) banks should not finance restaurants lacking indoor seating

(C) if the new fast-food place had indoor seating, it probably would have been successful

(D) a fast-food place on 10th Street is likely to fail if it has any outdoor seating

(E) the new fast-food place on 10th Street was a risky venture

18. In an island nature preserve, Common Eider nests are found in roughly equal numbers in highly concealing woody vegetation, wooden boxes, and open grasslands that do not conceal nests. Some Common Eiders lay their eggs in nests established by other Common Eiders, probably in order to locate them in an area that is maximally safe from predation. Although one would expect the nests concealed in woody vegetation to be most commonly selected by other females for laying their eggs, the female Common Eiders that lay their eggs in other birds' nests most commonly select established nests in wooden boxes.

Which one of the following, if true, would most help to explain why, in this nature preserve, Common Eiders that lay their eggs in other birds' nests most commonly select established nests in wooden boxes?

(A) Some Common Eiders that lay their eggs in nests established by other Common Eiders have been observed, in subsequent years, building nests of their own in the nature preserve.

(B) Established nests concealed in woody vegetation are difficult for Common Eiders to detect.

(C) Defensive behavior by nest builders can sometimes deter intruding Common Eiders.

(D) Virtually all of the island nature preserve consists of habitats that have been, at some point in the past, altered by humans.

(E) Foxes and other natural predators of the Common Eider are not uncommon in the island nature preserve.

GO ON TO THE NEXT PAGE.

19. Researcher: In an experiment, 500 families were given a medical self-help book, and 500 similar families were not. Over the next year, the average number of visits to doctors dropped by 20 percent for the families who had been given the book but remained unchanged for the other families. Since improved family health leads to fewer visits to doctors, the experiment indicates that having a medical self-help book in the home improves family health.

The reasoning in the researcher's argument is questionable in that

(A) it is possible that the families in the experiment who were not given a medical self-help book acquired medical self-help books on their own

(B) the families in the experiment could have gained access to medical self-help information outside of books

(C) a state of affairs could causally contribute to two or more different effects

(D) two different states of affairs could each causally contribute to the same effect even though neither causally contributes to the other

(E) certain states of affairs that lead families to visit the doctor less frequently could also make them more likely to have a medical self-help book in the home

20. Politician: Our government's Ministry of the Environment issues scientific assessments of the ecological impacts of industrial activities. However, these assessments are often inaccurate due to political pressures on the ministry. The government is now forming a Ministry of Health. Since the Ministry of Health will also be subject to political pressures in relation to health issues, it should not issue scientific assessments that relate to health issues.

Which one of the following principles, if valid, would most help to justify the politician's argument?

(A) If there was no need for scientific assessments of a set of issues before a government ministry responsible for those issues was formed, then those assessments are still unnecessary after the formation of the ministry.

(B) Scientific assessments should not be issued by government ministries unless they have very strong reason to believe that those assessments are accurate.

(C) Individuals and organizations should not exercise political pressure on government ministries that issue scientific assessments.

(D) A government ministry should issue scientific assessments of certain issues if that ministry can successfully resist political pressures to modify the contents of those assessments.

(E) The government ministry in charge of issuing assessments relating to health issues should firmly resist any political pressures regarding those assessments.

GO ON TO THE NEXT PAGE.

21. Farmer: Farming with artificial fertilizers, though more damaging to the environment than organic farming, allows more food to be grown on the same amount of land. If all farmers were to practice organic farming, they would be unable to produce enough food for Earth's growing population. Hence, if enough food is to be produced, the currently popular practice of organic farming must not spread any further.

The reasoning in the farmer's argument is most vulnerable to criticism on which one of the following grounds?

(A) It takes for granted that farming with artificial fertilizers is only slightly more damaging to the environment than organic farming is.

(B) It overlooks the possibility that even if the practice of organic farming continues to spread, many farmers will choose not to adopt it.

(C) It fails to consider the possibility that, at some points in human history, enough food was produced to feed Earth's population without the use of artificial fertilizers.

(D) It overlooks the possibility that a consequence that would surely follow if all farmers adopted the practice of organic farming would still ensue even if not all of them did.

(E) It takes for granted that damage to the environment due to the continued use of artificial fertilizers would not be detrimental to human health.

22. Although severing a motor nerve kills part of the nerve, it can regenerate, growing about 1 millimeter per day from the point of damage toward the muscle the nerve controlled. So, for example, a severed motor nerve that controlled a hand muscle requires a much longer time to regenerate if that nerve is severed at the shoulder rather than at the wrist. Furthermore, the growing cells require the original nerve sheath to guide them to the area that has lost function, but that sheath begins to disintegrate after about three months unless there is living nerve tissue within it.

The statements above, if true, most strongly support which one of the following?

(A) Doubling the speed at which new nerve cells grow will double the likelihood that a severed motor nerve will reach the muscle it had controlled.

(B) It is sometimes possible, once a nerve sheath has begun to disintegrate, to reverse or slow the process of disintegration.

(C) If a severed motor nerve does not regenerate successfully within three months after being severed, functioning cannot be restored to the muscle that the nerve had controlled.

(D) If living nerve tissue could be implanted and sustained within the original sheath of a severed motor nerve, the likelihood that the nerve will regenerate would increase in some cases.

(E) Without surgical intervention, a muscle that has lost function because of a severed motor nerve is unlikely to regain that function.

GO ON TO THE NEXT PAGE.

23. Male boto dolphins often carry objects such as weeds or sticks. Researchers first thought this was play behavior, but it is more likely to be a mating display. If it were play rather than a mating display, we would expect females and juveniles to engage in the behavior, but only adult males do.

The pattern of reasoning in the argument above is most similar to that in which one of the following arguments?

(A) If there is a lot of traffic today, then Phyllis will probably be late to the meeting. But I expect light traffic today. So in all likelihood Phyllis will arrive on time.

(B) I expect the arborist to determine that this tree is diseased. If the arborist finds that the tree is diseased, then the tree will definitely be cut down. So it is likely that the tree will be cut down.

(C) If the weather forecast called for heavy snow, then I would have expected Roy to cancel his trip to his mountain cabin. Indeed, Roy did cancel the trip. So it is likely that the forecast called for heavy snow.

(D) If construction of that building were on schedule, then I would expect the foundation to have been completed already. But work on the foundation has just started, so construction is probably behind schedule.

(E) If Tamika makes a big sale today, I would expect her to celebrate tonight. So, since Tamika will probably make a big sale today, she will probably celebrate tonight.

24. Andy Warhol's *Brillo Boxes* is a stack of boxes that are visually indistinguishable from the product packaging of an actual brand of scouring pads. Warhol's *Brillo Boxes* is considered a work of art, while an identical stack of ordinary boxes would not be considered a work of art. Therefore, it is not true that appearance alone entirely determines whether or not something is considered a work of art.

The argument proceeds by

(A) highlighting the differences between things that are believed to have a certain property and things that actually have that property

(B) demonstrating that an opposing argument relies on an ambiguity

(C) suggesting that two things that are indistinguishable from each other must be the same type of thing

(D) questioning the assumptions underlying a particular theory

(E) showing that something that would be impossible if a particular thesis were correct is actually true

25. Stallworth claims that she supported the proposal to build a new community center. If Henning also supported that proposal, it would have received government approval. Since the proposal did not gain government approval, Henning must have failed to back it, despite his claims to the contrary.

Which one of the following arguments is most similar in its flawed reasoning to the argument above?

(A) According to the TV news, the traffic accident occurred on Aylmer Street. But if the accident occurred on Aylmer Street, Morgan could not have witnessed it from his kitchen window. Thus, the newspaper report was mistaken in its claim that Morgan witnessed the accident from his kitchen window.

(B) According to the city government, 15 percent of city residents are behind on their property taxes. But according to a private institute, property taxes in the city are far higher than the national average for cities of that size. Thus it is the city government that is to blame for the high percentage of residents who are behind on their taxes.

(C) According to Kapoor, the hazardous-waste disposal site does not pose an imminent danger to the community. But according to Galindo, the disposal site is located on an unsuitable tract of land. Thus, if Galindo is correct, Kapoor's assessment is in error.

(D) According to Harris's political rivals, she consistently favors the interests of property developers. A good mayor must be willing to stand up to the city's powerful interests, including property developers. Harris is thus a poor choice for mayor.

(E) According to the latest government figures, the regional unemployment rate declined in the last six months. But the region lost thousands of manufacturing jobs in that period. The government's unemployment figures must therefore be inaccurate.

S T O P

IF YOU FINISH BEFORE TIME IS CALLED, YOU MAY CHECK YOUR WORK ON THIS SECTION ONLY.
DO NOT WORK ON ANY OTHER SECTION IN THE TEST.

SECTION II

Time—35 minutes

23 Questions

Directions: Each set of questions in this section is based on a scenario with a set of conditions. The questions are to be answered on the basis of what can be logically inferred from the scenario and conditions. For each question, choose the response that most accurately and completely answers the question and mark that response on your answer sheet.

Questions 1–6

Six speakers—Jacobs, Kennedy, Lewis, Martin, Navarro, and Ota—will lecture at an upcoming two-day conference, held on a Thursday and Friday. Lectures will be given at 1:00, 2:00, and 3:00 each day. Each speaker will lecture exactly once, and only one speaker will lecture at a time. The schedule for the conference must conform to the following conditions:

  Jacobs lectures at 1:00.
  Martin and Navarro lecture on the same day as each other.
  Lewis and Ota do not lecture on the same day as each other.
  If Lewis lectures on Friday, Lewis lectures at 1:00.

1. Which one of the following could be the schedule for the conference?

(A) Thursday: 1:00 Jacobs; 2:00 Kennedy; 3:00 Ota
     Friday: 1:00 Martin; 2:00 Navarro; 3:00 Lewis
(B) Thursday: 1:00 Jacobs; 2:00 Lewis; 3:00 Kennedy
     Friday: 1:00 Ota; 2:00 Martin; 3:00 Navarro
(C) Thursday: 1:00 Kennedy; 2:00 Lewis; 3:00 Martin
     Friday: 1:00 Jacobs; 2:00 Navarro; 3:00 Ota
(D) Thursday: 1:00 Lewis; 2:00 Kennedy; 3:00 Ota
     Friday: 1:00 Jacobs; 2:00 Martin; 3:00 Navarro
(E) Thursday: 1:00 Navarro; 2:00 Martin; 3:00 Ota
     Friday: 1:00 Lewis; 2:00 Jacobs; 3:00 Kennedy

GO ON TO THE NEXT PAGE.

2. If Martin lectures at 1:00, then any of the following could be true EXCEPT:

(A) Jacobs lectures on Thursday.
(B) Kennedy lectures on Friday.
(C) Lewis lectures on Friday.
(D) Martin lectures on Thursday.
(E) Navarro lectures on Friday.

3. Which one of the following is a pair of speakers who CANNOT lecture on the same day as each other?

(A) Jacobs and Navarro
(B) Jacobs and Ota
(C) Kennedy and Lewis
(D) Lewis and Martin
(E) Navarro and Ota

4. If Kennedy lectures at 3:00 on Friday, which one of the following must be true?

(A) Jacobs lectures at 1:00 on Thursday.
(B) Lewis lectures at 1:00 on Friday.
(C) Martin lectures at 1:00 on Thursday.
(D) Navarro lectures at 2:00 on Thursday.
(E) Ota lectures at 2:00 on Friday.

5. Which one of the following speakers CANNOT lecture at 1:00?

(A) Kennedy
(B) Lewis
(C) Martin
(D) Navarro
(E) Ota

6. Which one of the following, if substituted for the condition that Lewis and Ota do not lecture on the same day as each other, would have the same effect in determining the schedule for the conference?

(A) Jacobs and Kennedy lecture on the same day as each other.
(B) Kennedy and Ota lecture on the same day as each other.
(C) Navarro and Ota lecture on the same day as each other.
(D) Jacobs and Martin do not lecture on the same day as each other.
(E) Kennedy and Navarro do not lecture on the same day as each other.

GO ON TO THE NEXT PAGE.

Questions 7–12

An art auction will feature exactly six paintings, each by a different artist—Joysmith, Kahlo, Nieto, Rothko, Sugimoto, and Villa. Each painting will be auctioned separately, in an order consistent with the following:

    The Joysmith cannot be auctioned immediately before or immediately after the Villa.

    The Villa must be auctioned earlier than the Kahlo, and the Kahlo must be auctioned earlier than the Sugimoto.

    The Nieto must be auctioned second or third.

    The Rothko must be auctioned earlier than the Nieto.

7. The earliest that the Kahlo could be auctioned is

(A) first
(B) second
(C) third
(D) fourth
(E) fifth

GO ON TO THE NEXT PAGE.

8. The Joysmith CANNOT be auctioned

   (A) first
   (B) second
   (C) third
   (D) fourth
   (E) fifth

9. The Kahlo must be the fourth painting auctioned if which one of the following is true?

   (A) The Joysmith is auctioned fifth.
   (B) The Nieto is auctioned third.
   (C) The Rothko is auctioned second.
   (D) The Villa is auctioned first.
   (E) The Villa is auctioned second.

10. How many of the paintings are there that could be the one auctioned fifth?

    (A) one
    (B) two
    (C) three
    (D) four
    (E) five

11. If the Villa is auctioned fourth, then how many of the paintings are there that could be the one auctioned second?

    (A) five
    (B) four
    (C) three
    (D) two
    (E) one

12. If the Sugimoto is auctioned earlier than the Joysmith, then which one of the following must be true?

    (A) The first painting auctioned is the Rothko.
    (B) The second painting auctioned is the Rothko.
    (C) The second painting auctioned is the Villa.
    (D) The third painting auctioned is the Nieto.
    (E) The fourth painting auctioned is the Kahlo.

GO ON TO THE NEXT PAGE.

Questions 13–17

Every year, a mining company dispatches an engineering team to work for three months at Grayson mine and for three months at Krona mine. All six of the months occur from March to November. In months when it is not at a mine, the team works at company headquarters. The team's schedule also conforms to the following constraints:

The team must work for at least one month at headquarters between any two months working at different mines.

The team cannot work at the same mine for more than two months in a row.

The team must work at Grayson mine in August.

The team must work at Krona mine in October.

13. Which one of the following could be an acceptable schedule for the team from June through October?

(A)   June: Grayson; July: Grayson; August: Grayson; September: headquarters; October: Krona

(B)   June: Grayson; July: headquarters; August: Grayson; September: headquarters; October: Krona

(C)   June: Grayson; July: headquarters; August: Krona; September: headquarters; October: Krona

(D)   June: headquarters; July: Grayson; August: Grayson; September: headquarters; October: Grayson

(E)   June: Krona; July: Krona; August: Grayson; September: headquarters; October: Krona

GO ON TO THE NEXT PAGE.

14. Which one of the following is a month in which the team must work at Krona mine?

   (A)   March
   (B)   May
   (C)   June
   (D)   September
   (E)   November

15. Which one of the following must be true?

   (A)   The team works at Grayson mine in June.
   (B)   The team works at Grayson mine in July.
   (C)   The team works at headquarters in June.
   (D)   The team works at headquarters in September.
   (E)   The team works at Krona mine in May.

16. If the team works at Grayson mine in May, which one of the following could be true?

   (A)   The team works at Grayson mine in March.
   (B)   The team works at Grayson mine in April.
   (C)   The team works at Grayson mine in June.
   (D)   The team works at Krona mine in April.
   (E)   The team works at Krona mine in June.

17. If the team works at Grayson mine in July, which one of the following could be true?

   (A)   The team works at Grayson mine in April.
   (B)   The team works at Grayson mine in June.
   (C)   The team works at headquarters in May.
   (D)   The team works at Krona mine in March.
   (E)   The team works at Krona mine in June.

GO ON TO THE NEXT PAGE.

Questions 18–23

A medical clinic is assigning doctors to shifts for the next seven days, Sunday through Saturday, with exactly one doctor assigned to each day. Six doctors—Graham, Herrera, Koppel, Leedom, Nelson, and Park—will be assigned, each doctor assigned to at least one day, subject to the following conditions:

The doctor assigned to Sunday must also be assigned to Saturday.

Graham must be assigned to exactly one day.

The day to which Graham is assigned must be immediately before or immediately after a day to which Koppel is assigned.

Herrera cannot be assigned to a day immediately before or immediately after a day to which Nelson is assigned.

Park must be assigned to Tuesday.

18. Which one of the following is an acceptable assignment for the doctors, listed in order from Sunday through Saturday?

(A)   Herrera, Graham, Park, Leedom, Nelson, Koppel, Herrera

(B)   Herrera, Leedom, Park, Nelson, Graham, Koppel, Leedom

(C)   Herrera, Nelson, Park, Graham, Koppel, Leedom, Herrera

(D)   Leedom, Herrera, Park, Koppel, Graham, Nelson, Leedom

(E)   Leedom, Park, Herrera, Graham, Koppel, Nelson, Leedom

GO ON TO THE NEXT PAGE.

19. If Nelson is assigned to Sunday, which one of the following must be true?

   (A)   Herrera is assigned to Wednesday.
   (B)   Herrera is assigned to Thursday.
   (C)   Koppel is assigned to Thursday.
   (D)   Koppel is assigned to Friday.
   (E)   Leedom is assigned to Wednesday.

20. If Koppel is assigned to Thursday, then any of the following could be true EXCEPT:

   (A)   Herrera is assigned to Friday.
   (B)   Leedom is assigned to Sunday.
   (C)   Leedom is assigned to Wednesday.
   (D)   Nelson is assigned to Sunday.
   (E)   Nelson is assigned to Wednesday.

21. If Leedom is assigned to Wednesday, which one of the following could be true?

   (A)   Graham is assigned to Monday.
   (B)   Herrera is assigned to Sunday.
   (C)   Koppel is assigned to Friday.
   (D)   Nelson is assigned to Sunday.
   (E)   Nelson is assigned to Thursday.

22. If Leedom is assigned to Thursday, which one of the following must be true?

   (A)   Graham is assigned to Monday.
   (B)   Herrera is assigned to Wednesday.
   (C)   Herrera is assigned to Friday.
   (D)   Koppel is assigned to Sunday.
   (E)   Nelson is assigned to Monday.

23. Any of the following could be true EXCEPT:

   (A)   Graham is assigned to Friday.
   (B)   Herrera is assigned to Sunday.
   (C)   Herrera is assigned to Friday.
   (D)   Koppel is assigned to Sunday.
   (E)   Leedom is assigned to Friday.

S T O P

IF YOU FINISH BEFORE TIME IS CALLED, YOU MAY CHECK YOUR WORK ON THIS SECTION ONLY.
DO NOT WORK ON ANY OTHER SECTION IN THE TEST.

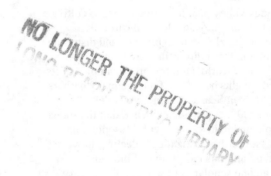

SECTION III

Time—35 minutes

26 Questions

<u>Directions</u>: Each set of questions in this section is based on a single passage or a pair of passages. The questions are to be answered on the basis of what is <u>stated</u> or <u>implied</u> in the passage or pair of passages. For some questions, more than one of the choices could conceivably answer the question. However, you are to choose the <u>best</u> answer; that is, choose the response that most accurately and completely answers the question and mark that response on your answer sheet.

Along with Egypt and Sumer, the third major early Bronze Age civilization was the Indus Valley civilization, which flourished from 2600 B.C. to 900 B.C. In geographic size, the Indus Valley
(5) civilization was the largest ancient urban civilization, bigger than pharaonic Egypt. Centered on the Indus River and the now dry Ghaggar-Hakra River, it comprised about 1,400 settlements across what is now Pakistan, Afghanistan, and northwestern India.
(10) The Indus Valley civilization was long considered archaeologically uninteresting because of its ordinary urban architecture and lack of palaces or citadels, but recent excavations show the civilization to be without parallel in history, displaying characteristics not
(15) elsewhere united in a single civilization.
The Indus Valley people, masters of urban planning, built brick cities on flood-proof terraces with grids of long, straight streets and the first urban sewer systems, made of masonry. No signs of dominant
(20) rulers have been found, and the cities' living quarters show little sign of class distinction, suggesting that their system of government was, at least in part, democratic. The civilization also apparently thrived without armies—there is, for example, no evidence of
(25) weapon production.
The Indus Valley people were the first to cultivate rice and cotton, and they developed a carefully organized agricultural system to produce and distribute food. In addition, the Indus Valley civilization was
(30) one of the ancient world's top traders. Examples of its standardized weights have been found in many harbors around the Arabian Sea, and Sumerian tablets inscribed in 2300 B.C. provide evidence that the Indus Valley people maintained trade with Mesopotamia.
(35) The causes of the civilization's decline, however, are not certain, and this has produced the most contention among scholars. A long-standing theory, one that today still inhabits history books, was proposed by British archaeologist Mortimer Wheeler
(40) in the 1920s and points to a final massacre by marauding Indo-Aryan invaders. But, in addition to a lack of written evidence of such an event in any ancient Indian records, there is no archaeological evidence of battles within the cities. In fact, new
(45) excavations show that Indo-Aryans were not even in the region at the time the massacre was alleged to have taken place. Archaeological evidence also shows a later resurgence of the civilization a substantial distance to the south of its original location. This
(50) suggests that the Indus Valley people most likely relocated for catastrophic environmental reasons, with

the large empire disintegrating into many regional cultures. Severe drought, of which there is evidence, may have made some lands unfarmable. Without
(55) enough grain to feed the large urban populations, many of the Indus Valley civilization's large cities would probably have been abandoned. Or, a massive earthquake in this seismically volatile region may have changed the course of rivers and disrupted many cities,
(60) spurring a migration of refugees to the countryside.

1. Which one of the following most accurately states the main point of the passage?

(A) Recent evidence sheds new light on the Indus Valley civilization and calls into question some of the views held previously by archaeologists regarding its significance and decline.
(B) Bronze Age civilizations, including that of the Indus Valley, have not been properly recognized for their cultural achievements.
(C) The Indus Valley civilization played an important role in the evolution of democracy and modern agriculture.
(D) The Indus Valley civilization is a historically significant culture, but there is not enough evidence to draw legitimate conclusions about the cultural practices of its people.
(E) Certain long-held assumptions about the decline of the Indus Valley civilization exemplify how scholars can be led to incorrect conclusions by incomplete data.

2. Which one of the following is NOT cited in the passage as a characteristic of the Indus Valley civilization?

(A) It was geographically the largest of the major Bronze Age civilizations.
(B) Its people cultivated rice.
(C) Its people were generally nomadic.
(D) It was a major trader.
(E) It was spread across an area that is now part of three nations.

GO ON TO THE NEXT PAGE.

3. Based on the passage, which one of the following most accurately describes the author's stance regarding Wheeler's theory?

(A) enthusiastic appreciation of its contributions to the field of archaeology

(B) grudging approval of those aspects of the theory that have not been refuted by recent research

(C) slight disagreement with its assumptions, mixed with respect for its venerable status

(D) offhanded dismissal of it as a theory not worthy of scholarly attention

(E) unambiguous rejection of it in light of newly conducted excavations

4. Which one of the following is cited in the passage as evidence that directly counters Wheeler's theory?

(A) The Indus Valley is a seismically volatile region.

(B) There are no findings that indicate battles within Bronze Age Indus Valley cities.

(C) There is evidence of severe drought in the Indus Valley at the time of the Bronze Age.

(D) No signs of dominant rulers of the Indus Valley civilization have been found at excavation sites.

(E) The Indus Valley people practiced agriculture.

5. The author would be most likely to agree with which one of the following statements?

(A) Because the Indus Valley region is prone to earthquakes, it is most likely that an earthquake destroyed the Indus Valley civilization.

(B) Only a disaster as catastrophic as an earthquake would have caused the demise of a civilization as sophisticated as the Indus Valley civilization.

(C) Archaeologists' understanding of the decline of the Indus Valley civilization would benefit from a search for signs of earthquake damage in its cities.

(D) The cities of the Indus Valley civilization should have been better prepared for the possibility of a major earthquake.

(E) The demise of the Indus Valley civilization was most likely caused by the catastrophic alteration of the courses of its major rivers.

6. The author would be most likely to agree with which one of the following statements about archaeological investigations into the Indus Valley civilization?

(A) Archaeological data on the civilization were controlled by a small group of scholars for many years, leading to unfounded conclusions.

(B) It is only in recent years that scholars have gathered evidence sufficient to enable them to reach credible conclusions regarding the civilization.

(C) The Sumerian tablets that provide evidence of trade with the civilization contain the only known references to the civilization in ancient written records.

(D) While an adequate amount of archaeological data on the civilization has existed for many decades, most of it has been misinterpreted.

(E) The most recent archaeological investigations into the civilization are part of a broader trend in archaeology to avoid overreliance on written evidence.

GO ON TO THE NEXT PAGE.

Film scholar David Bordwell refers to the years 1917–1960 as the classical era of filmmaking in Hollywood. Bordwell defines the era's style as being governed by straightforward narrative considerations,
(5) i.e., the need to follow well-defined characters through a chronological sequence of events, or plot. The technical elements of filmmaking—camera movement, lighting, editing, and sound—are all employed to tell a realistic story, one in which the world of the story is
(10) self-sufficient and recognizably related to our own. Devices that draw attention to the film as film rather than to the story are avoided.

Within this definition, the musical films of the 1930s are anomalous in that they interrupt narrative to
(15) present musical performances only tangentially related to the plot. In one film directed by Busby Berkeley, for example, a scene begins with a shot of an audience watching a singer. The singer's face then fills the screen—a natural enough transition—but this image
(20) soon dissolves into a fanciful sequence consisting of various aerial views of city life. Although the sequence illustrates the song being sung, it does not contribute to the story Berkeley tells between musical numbers. In such sequences, filmmaking techniques
(25) are used not to advance a narrative but as a respite from narrative; the people we see are not characters in a plot but rather are abstracted figures; editing and camera movement function not to help tell a story but to manipulate images into intricate patterns. Can the
(30) musical—in which such differently motivated and constructed sequences abut so closely—fit comfortably within Bordwell's definition of the classical style?

Bordwell's response is that the musical, no less than comedy or melodrama (two other staples of the
(35) classical era), evolved from popular live theater. The musical's conventions, Bordwell argues, cue viewers to expect a different structure—alternating narrative scenes and self-contained performances—from that of other genres, a structure that audiences are prepared
(40) for and thus accept as "realistic." But raising the issue of genre does not disguise the fact that Bordwell stretches the definition of the term "realism," for there is still the problem exemplified in films such as Berkeley's by the fact that the musical performances
(45) are not merely self-contained but self-absorbed—the selfish aesthetic of the interlude isn't intended to advance the plot but instead to draw attention to its own artistic expertise. Even the viewer aware of the film's genre cannot remain entirely unfazed by the
(50) break in the film's "reality." Bordwell too quickly dismisses the fact that watching a film is a perceptual act and not an academic exercise in pigeonholing genres. Because knowledge of genre is acquired, it would be worthwhile for scholars like Bordwell to
(55) first consider how viewers process cinematic images and eventually come to accept them as conventions before generalizing about the realism of certain film styles.

7. Which one of the following most accurately states the main point of the passage?

(A) Despite some evidence to the contrary, Bordwell's definition of the classical style of filmmaking is borne out by a more careful examination of Hollywood film genres such as the musical.

(B) Contrary to Bordwell's claims, the musicals of the 1930s such as Busby Berkeley's are not realistic because they do not depict events in chronological order.

(C) Because film genres such as the musical evolved from popular theatrical forms, it can be argued that they fit comfortably within Bordwell's definition of the classical style of filmmaking.

(D) The films of Busby Berkeley do not meet the requirements of Bordwell's definition of the classical style of filmmaking and therefore cannot be considered examples of the classical style of filmmaking.

(E) The fact that Bordwell's definition of the classical style of filmmaking is obliged to treat musicals of the 1930s as realistic, despite compelling evidence to the contrary, illustrates the misguided nature of Bordwell's approach.

8. The passage identifies each of the following as a component of Bordwell's definition of the classical style of filmmaking EXCEPT:

(A) avoidance of filmmaking techniques that call attention to the film medium

(B) creation and presentation of clearly defined characters

(C) portrayal of a self-sufficient and relatively realistic world

(D) use of nonnarrative interludes between episodes of plot

(E) depiction of a chronological sequence of events

9. The author uses the term "realistic" throughout the passage to refer to which one of the following qualities of a film?

(A) the quality that allows the narrative structure to convey the story being told in the film

(B) the quality that allows the world of the story told in the film to resemble actual life

(C) the quality that allows the technical elements of filmmaking to contribute to the story being told in the film

(D) the quality that allows audiences to determine easily the genre to which the film belongs

(E) the quality that allows the film to employ a variety of narrative structures to tell a story

GO ON TO THE NEXT PAGE.

10. Which one of the following most accurately describes the organization of the passage?

(A) The author states a scholar's thesis, counters the thesis with an example, summarizes the scholar's response to the example, points out a problem with the response, and criticizes the focus of the scholar's research.

(B) The author takes issue with a scholar's thesis, provides an example in support of a counterthesis, summarizes the scholar's response to the example, and argues in favor of replacing the scholar's thesis with the counterthesis.

(C) The author states a scholar's thesis, illustrates the thesis with an example, summarizes the scholar's interpretation of the example, points out a problem with the interpretation, and makes a suggestion for modifying the interpretation.

(D) The author takes issue with a scholar's thesis, provides an example illustrating the drawbacks of the thesis, summarizes the scholar's response to the example, points out a problem with the response, and offers a new thesis to replace the scholar's thesis.

(E) The author states a scholar's thesis, presents the results of research supporting the thesis, counters the results with an example, summarizes the scholar's response to the example, acknowledges the legitimacy of the response, but suggests that further research is needed to settle the matter.

11. The author of the passage would most likely agree with which one of the following statements?

(A) Busby Berkeley's films are unique among musicals in that their performance sequences do not contribute to their narratives.

(B) The use of technical elements in films of the classical era was usually very simplistic.

(C) The film genres popular in the classical era were all derived from noncinematic popular entertainment forms.

(D) Audiences learn to accept certain cinematic images as conventions primarily through repeated exposure to such images.

(E) Most musical films of the 1930s concentrated on telling realistic stories.

12. The narrative structure of which one of the following hypothetical novels is most closely parallel to that of the musical films of the 1930s, as that genre is described by the author of the passage?

(A) a novel that depicts a series of events, moving from one event to another without providing information necessary for understanding the context or chronology of the events

(B) a novel that follows a number of characters who do not know one another, depicting a single event in each of their lives and concluding with a final event that unites all of the characters

(C) a novel that follows a number of characters who all reside in the same town, depicting a single event in each of their lives that together combine to form a portrait of a typical day in the town

(D) a novel that follows a protagonist through a series of events, pausing throughout to provide information relevant to the events by means of fanciful flashbacks to the protagonist's youth

(E) a novel that follows a protagonist through the events of a single day, pausing throughout for stylistically elaborate sections expressing the protagonist's thoughts and fantasies about life in general

13. Which one of the following, if true, would most call into question the position of Bordwell described in the first two sentences of the last paragraph?

(A) evidence that reviewers of musical films in the 1930s generally praised the films' unrealistic elements

(B) evidence that audiences went to musical films in the 1930s primarily to enjoy the musical performances

(C) evidence that viewers of musical films in the 1930s all experienced these films in the same way, whether or not they had previously been exposed to musicals

(D) evidence that audience members tend to have longer attention spans when watching films with whose genres they are unfamiliar

(E) evidence that the musicals presented in popular live theater before the 1930s are stylistically very similar to the musical films of the 1930s

GO ON TO THE NEXT PAGE.

Passage A

The legal system rests on the assumption that people use conscious deliberation when deciding how to act—that is, in the absence of external duress, people freely decide how to act. But behaviors—even
(5) high-level behaviors—can take place in the absence of free will. For example, someone with a neurological disorder might form a facial expression without *choosing* to do so.

The crucial legal question is whether *all* of our
(10) actions are fundamentally beyond our control or whether some little bit of you is "free" to choose, independent of the rules of biology. After all, as neurologists tell us, there is no spot in the brain that is not densely interconnected with—and driven by—
(15) other brain parts. And that suggests that no part is independent and therefore "free."

One thing seems clear: if free will *does* exist, it has little room in which to operate. It can at best be a small factor riding on top of vast neural networks
(20) shaped by genes and environment. In fact, free will may end up being so small that we eventually think about bad decision-making in the same way we think about any physical affliction.

Blameworthiness should thus be removed from
(25) the legal argot. It is a backward-looking concept that demands the impossible task of untangling the hopelessly complex web of genetics and environment in order to isolate a factor of free will that may or may not exist. Instead of debating culpability, the legal
(30) system has to become forward looking, and address how an accused lawbreaker is likely to behave in the future.

Passage B

Here is a paradox: if people lack free will, then how can the law be moved away from what seems to
(35) be a deeply entrenched reliance on blame-related concepts? Rational arguments will only get you so far.

Clinical research indicates that people will often continue to make moral judgments even when they are conditioned to think that human behavior is determined
(40) by physical processes. The blaming urge is deeply rooted in the human psyche, and I have considerable doubt that any amount of scientific evidence can remove it from our criminal justice processes.

We have, of course, tried this before.
(45) Rehabilitation was widely accepted by criminal justice experts in the mid-twentieth century. But public support waned, and a retributive backlash occurred in the 1970s and 1980s. Criminal behavior may be a matter of biology, not choice, but the public seems
(50) unwilling to incorporate this idea into the law.

My sense is that blaming performs some useful social function, even if it is in some way "false." Blaming seems too intrinsically a part of the social life of human beings for me to see it as a worthless
(55) appendage that can be harmlessly amputated. As the criminal justice system confronts the challenges of brain science, it should also seek a better understanding of why people blame and try to continue to respect the underlying social needs.

14. Both passages are primarily concerned with answering which one of the following questions?

(A) Does the public support rehabilitation over retribution as the purpose of criminal justice?
(B) Is the existence of free will compatible with the findings of brain science?
(C) Does the legal system require the assumption that people choose freely?
(D) Should the concept of blame be removed from criminal justice procedures?
(E) Is criminal behavior comparable to a physical affliction?

15. Which one of the following most accurately describes the attitude of the author of passage B toward the type of argument presented in passage A?

(A) sympathy with the premises, accompanied by doubts about the feasibility of the policy those premises are used to support.
(B) intellectual acceptance, coupled with fear of the consequences if such acceptance becomes widespread
(C) forceful rejection, both of the argument's conclusion and one or more of the premises on which it is based
(D) studied neutrality, with regard both to the conclusion and to the steps by which it is arrived at
(E) sympathy with the conclusion amid doubt that it follows from the premises

16. The meaning of the phrase "forward looking" (line 30) as it is used in passage A is most closely related to which one of the following concepts in passage B?

(A) entrenched (line 35)
(B) rational (line 36)
(C) conditioned (line 39)
(D) rehabilitation (line 45)
(E) backlash (line 47)

GO ON TO THE NEXT PAGE.

17. It is most likely that the authors of the passages would disagree with each other about the truth of which one of the following statements?

(A) A significant portion of people's choices are made freely.
(B) If free will does not exist, criminal law should not assign blame for any action.
(C) People should be imprisoned for actions from which they are not free to refrain.
(D) Actions that are completely determined by physical processes are not free.
(E) It is easy to eliminate the concept of blame from everyday life.

18. Which one of the following, if true, would cast the most doubt on the argument in passage B?

(A) A new drug enables patients with a particular neurological disorder to exercise apparent control over their symptoms.
(B) In patients with a particular brain injury, the two hemispheres of the brain become causally isolated from one another.
(C) Subjects in a psychological experiment display random responses to a repeated stimulus.
(D) Some governments restrict the legal concept of blame to cases of disobedience to the authorities.
(E) There are societies that have no concept of blame.

19. Which one of the following conforms to the policy advocated by the author of passage A but not advocated by the author of passage B?

(A) Parents should refrain from words and actions that could cause their children to feel ashamed of behavior that the parents regard as socially unacceptable.
(B) Prosecutors should be allowed to exclude jurors whose beliefs about free will make them unwilling to assign blame to anyone who is accused of a crime.
(C) The admissibility of expert testimony regarding a defendant's state of mind should be subject to strict guidelines.
(D) The findings of brain science should be viewed with suspicion, since they imply that the brain scientists themselves did not arrive at them by conscious deliberation.
(E) Courts should be allowed to consider a convicted criminal's motives to determine the likelihood that the criminal will offend again, but not to determine degree of culpability.

GO ON TO THE NEXT PAGE.

Physicists posit that at first our universe was infinitesimally small and infinitely hot and dense. It then underwent a period of extremely rapid, massive inflation (the Big Bang), and it has since continued to
(5) expand and cool.

According to physicists Sean Carroll and Jennifer Chen, the Big Bang was not a unique event; events like it happen periodically over an incredibly vast time scale. This is based on the suggestion of some
(10) physicists that the Big Bang was the beginning of our universe as we know it, but not the beginning of a larger Universe—or "multiverse"—that encompasses everything, including that which we can never see because it is beyond our "cosmic bubble."

(15) Carroll and Chen were initially interested in why time flows in only one direction. In physics the flow of time is captured by the second law of thermodynamics, which implies that entropy—a measure of total disorder—naturally increases with time. Entropy
(20) increases because there are more ways for a system to be disordered than for it to be ordered. Therefore, if change occurs, it is more likely to be change toward greater disorder. For example, in a moderately orderly room, if one moves an object in the room randomly,
(25) there are many more places one can put it that will make the room less orderly than there are places that will make it more orderly. So if, over time, objects in the room are continually moved randomly, it is most likely that the room will get increasingly disordered.

(30) While the Big Bang process and what followed obey the second law of thermodynamics, it is a mystery why there should have been a small, hot, and dense universe to begin with. Such a low entropy universe is an extremely unlikely configuration, not
(35) what scientists would expect from a randomly occurring initial condition. Carroll and Chen's innovation is to argue that the most common initial condition is actually likely to resemble cold, empty space—not an obviously favorable starting point for
(40) the onset of inflation.

Recent research has shown that even empty space has faint traces of energy that fluctuate on the subatomic scale. Physicists Jaume Garriga and Alexander Vilenkin have suggested that these
(45) fluctuations can generate their own big bangs in tiny areas widely separated in time and space. Carroll and Chen take our universe, and others, to be such fluctuations in a high entropy multiverse.

On this view, while the initial state that produced
(50) our universe would appear to be, taken by itself, a highly improbable one, in the vastness of the multiverse the creation of our universe is not that unlikely. Indeed it is likely not even a unique event.

20. Which one of the following most accurately states the main idea of the passage?

(A) Carroll and Chen theorize that our universe is the result of an energy fluctuation in a high entropy multiverse.
(B) According to Carroll and Chen, entropy increases because there are more ways for a system to be disordered than for it to be ordered.
(C) Carroll and Chen challenge the prevailing view of physicists that our universe underwent a period of extremely rapid, massive inflation.
(D) According to Carroll and Chen, a small, hot, and dense configuration is unlikely as a random initial condition for a universe.
(E) Carroll and Chen posit that our universe is one of many universes in an all-encompassing multiverse.

21. Which one of the following comes closest to capturing what the term "cosmic bubble" means in the last sentence of the second paragraph?

(A) all-encompassing larger universe
(B) universe contained in the multiverse
(C) inflation following a big bang
(D) theoretical preconceptions
(E) low entropy state

22. The author's stance toward Carroll and Chen's theory is most accurately characterized as that of

(A) an ardent adversary
(B) a dismissive critic
(C) a disinterested skeptic
(D) a sympathetic reporter
(E) a zealous proponent

23. The claim in the fourth paragraph that an initial condition is likely to resemble cold, empty space is most strongly supported by information in the

(A) first paragraph
(B) second paragraph
(C) third paragraph
(D) fifth paragraph
(E) sixth paragraph

GO ON TO THE NEXT PAGE.

24. The author's reference to a suggestion by Garriga and Vilenkin in the fifth paragraph primarily serves to

   (A) question a presupposition of the Big Bang theory
   (B) raise a potential objection to Carroll and Chen's theory
   (C) illustrate an implication of Carroll and Chen's theory
   (D) show how a puzzle raised by Carroll and Chen is resolved within Carroll and Chen's theory
   (E) suggest an alternative explanation of the evidence upon which Carroll and Chen's theory is based

25. The primary purpose of the passage is to

   (A) draw novel consequences from an established principle
   (B) challenge a dominant point of view
   (C) chronicle the history of a dispute
   (D) adjudicate between two theories
   (E) give the rationale for a theory

26. It can be inferred from the passage that the author presumes which one of the following to be true?

   (A) The multiverse originated in a big bang.
   (B) The initial state of our universe resembles cold, empty space.
   (C) A hot and dense state is a state of low entropy.
   (D) The multiverse is part of a larger system of multiverses.
   (E) The second law of thermodynamics was formulated to answer a question about time.

S T O P

IF YOU FINISH BEFORE TIME IS CALLED, YOU MAY CHECK YOUR WORK ON THIS SECTION ONLY.
DO NOT WORK ON ANY OTHER SECTION IN THE TEST.

SECTION IV
Time—35 minutes
25 Questions

Directions: Each question in this section is based on the reasoning presented in a brief passage. In answering the questions, you should not make assumptions that are by commonsense standards implausible, superfluous, or incompatible with the passage. For some questions, more than one of the choices could conceivably answer the question. However, you are to choose the best answer; that is, choose the response that most accurately and completely answers the question and mark that response on your answer sheet.

1. Researcher: It is widely believed that, given its northerly latitude, England's mild winters must be due to the Gulf Stream, which brings warm water flowing northeastward across the Atlantic Ocean. But this belief is mistaken. While it is true that the Gulf Stream brings tropical water to England, in the Pacific Ocean the analogous Kuroshio Current brings tropical water only as far north as Oregon. Yet North America's west coast has mild winters well north of that point.

    Which one of the following most accurately expresses the conclusion drawn in the researcher's argument?

    (A)   It is widely believed that England's mild winters must be due to the Gulf Stream.
    (B)   The belief that England's mild winters must be due to the Gulf Stream is mistaken.
    (C)   It is true that the Gulf Stream brings tropical water to England.
    (D)   In the Pacific Ocean, the Kuroshio Current brings tropical water only as far north as Oregon.
    (E)   North America's west coast has mild winters well north of Oregon.

2. Edgar: Nurses who have been specially trained in administering anesthetics should be allowed to anesthetize patients without having to do so under a doctor's supervision. After all, anesthesia has gotten remarkably safe in recent decades.

    Janet: Although it's true that nurse anesthetists receive excellent training, only doctors have the broader medical training to handle the rare emergencies that can arise.

    The dialogue provides the most support for the claim that Edgar and Janet disagree over whether

    (A)   nurses should ever be allowed to anesthetize patients
    (B)   emergencies that can develop from anesthesia are rare
    (C)   nurses should be given more training in administering anesthetics
    (D)   the safety of anesthesia has improved in recent decades
    (E)   the administration of anesthetics by a nurse should always be supervised by a doctor

3. Consumer: A new law requires all cigarette packaging to display health warnings, disturbing pictures of smoking-related diseases, and no logos. This law will not affect the smoking habits of most people who smoke cigarettes regularly, since most of these people rarely look at the packaging when they take out a cigarette.

    The conclusion of the consumer's argument follows logically if which one of the following is assumed?

    (A)   If implementing certain regulations on the packaging of cigarettes would affect the smoking habits of those who smoke cigarettes regularly, those regulations should be implemented.
    (B)   If those who regularly smoke cigarettes look at disturbing pictures of smoking-related diseases frequently, it is likely to affect their smoking habits.
    (C)   Almost all people who regularly smoke cigarettes are already familiar with the risks that smoking poses to their health.
    (D)   The new packaging cannot affect the smoking habits of people who regularly smoke cigarettes unless they frequently look at the packaging when taking out cigarettes.
    (E)   Most people who regularly smoke cigarettes would be unable to describe the logo of their usual brand of cigarettes if asked to do so.

GO ON TO THE NEXT PAGE.

4. Warner: Until recently, most competitive swimmers were high school or university students. Now, more and more competitive swimmers are continuing well beyond their university years. Clearly, better training regimens have allowed today's competitive swimmers to stay fitter longer than swimmers of the past.

 Young: Not necessarily. No one has the time to both be a competitive swimmer and hold an outside job. But unlike in the past, today's competitive swimmers can make a living at their sport.

Young responds to Warner's argument by

(A) attempting to demonstrate that the evidence Warner advances actually undermines Warner's conclusion

(B) presenting a counterexample in order to weaken the evidence offered in support of Warner's conclusion

(C) arguing that a condition that Warner takes to be sufficient to account for a phenomenon is necessary but not sufficient

(D) maintaining that the evidence presented in support of Warner's conclusion presupposes the truth of that conclusion

(E) offering an alternative to Warner's explanation of a certain phenomenon

5. Businessperson: Brenner and Chen are the only applicants who have the qualifications we require. But Brenner has a history of not getting along with coworkers, so we should hire Chen.

Which one of the following arguments is most similar in its reasoning to the businessperson's argument?

(A) Jennifer has long been interested in visiting the historical sites in Mexico and Peru. The cost of traveling to these countries is currently very low. So she should book a trip now rather than continue to put it off.

(B) Jennifer has been planning to visit the historical sites in either Mexico or Peru. Floods have made it difficult to get to the historical sites in Peru. So she should visit the sites in Mexico.

(C) Jennifer would like to visit historical sites in either Mexico or Peru on her next vacation. This might be her only opportunity to take this sort of vacation. So Jennifer should choose the destination that she finds most interesting, regardless of cost.

(D) Jennifer has been planning to visit historical sites in either Mexico or Peru. Travel to Mexico and Peru is currently inexpensive. So she should instead plan to visit both.

(E) Jennifer would like to visit historical sites in Mexico and Peru. Travel to Mexico is currently cheaper than to Peru. So she should visit the historical sites in Mexico now and visit the sites in Peru at a later date.

6. Psychologist: Thinking can occur without language. Researchers have demonstrated that three-month-old infants, who obviously have no knowledge of language, can detect anomalies in pictures—in a picture displaying a human face with three eyes, for example. The infants probably compare this picture with an internal representation of a typical human face. Thus, a thought of a typical human face must exist in the infants' minds.

The statement that a thought of a typical human face must exist in the infants' minds plays which one of the following roles in the psychologist's argument?

(A) It is a conclusion drawn and used in turn as a premise to support a more general conclusion.

(B) It is attributed to certain researchers as the main conclusion of their reasoning.

(C) It is the main point of the psychologist's argument.

(D) It is used to refute the claim that infants have no knowledge of language.

(E) It states the hypothesis to be explained by the psychologist's argument.

7. Nutritionist: Contrary to popular belief, a high-calcium diet does not prevent osteoporosis (decrease in bone density). Rather, a low-protein diet with an abundance of fruits and vegetables and a minimum quantity of meat and dairy products is essential for the prevention of the condition. Weight-bearing exercise, such as walking or climbing stairs, is also essential, since bones thicken when they withstand regular resistance.

Each of the following, if true, would support the nutritionist's view EXCEPT:

(A) Astronauts who have lived in the weightless environment of space have exhibited decreases in bone density despite vigorous physical activity.

(B) Certain medical therapies that do not involve special diets can be effective means of preventing osteoporosis.

(C) Populations in countries with the lowest per capita rates of protein consumption have some of the lowest incidences of osteoporosis.

(D) Arctic peoples, who consume large amounts of calcium, exhibit one of the highest rates of osteoporosis in the world.

(E) The incidence of osteoporosis is unusually low among strict vegetarians with low-protein diets.

GO ON TO THE NEXT PAGE.

8. Quartzbrook Farms wanted to test all of its cattle for a rare disease so it could export beef to a country that requires such testing. However, the government of Quartzbrook's country prohibited it from testing its cattle, on the grounds that there is no scientific evidence that the risk posed by the disease justifies such testing and that the public could be misled into thinking that the testing was scientifically warranted if Quartzbrook performed the tests.

The government's prohibition of testing is most at odds with which one of the following principles?

(A) Governments can rightfully require product testing deemed necessary to protect public safety but cannot rightfully prohibit testing even if such testing is not justified by the risk involved.

(B) Governments should seek to determine when product safety testing is justified by the risk posed and should provide this information to companies that are considering such testing.

(C) A government should not allow a company to perform unnecessary product safety tests if that company's doing so will give consumers the impression that such tests should be performed.

(D) A government should not spend taxpayers' money performing product safety tests if the risk posed by the products does not justify the expense of the tests.

(E) It is fair for a country's government to require foreign companies to test the products they export to that country as long as it requires domestic companies to perform the same tests.

9. Office manager: Every vacation an office worker takes significantly reduces the psychological exhaustion experienced on the job. Therefore, to reduce the amount of psychological exhaustion as much as possible over the course of a year, office workers should divide their vacation time into several short vacations spaced throughout the year, rather than into one or two long vacations.

The office manager's argument is most vulnerable to criticism on which one of the following grounds?

(A) It takes for granted that each short vacation taken by an office worker during a year reduces the psychological exhaustion experienced on the job by an equal amount.

(B) It overlooks the possibility that there are methods office workers can employ to reduce the amount of psychological exhaustion experienced on the job that are as effective as taking vacations.

(C) It overlooks the possibility that individual office workers may differ substantially in the extent to which taking vacations reduces the amount of psychological exhaustion they experience on the job.

(D) It fails to consider that for office workers the total amount of vacation time taken over the course of a year may have a much greater effect on the amount of psychological exhaustion experienced on the job than does the number of vacations taken during the year.

(E) It fails to consider that a long vacation may reduce the psychological exhaustion an office worker experiences on the job much more than a short vacation does.

GO ON TO THE NEXT PAGE.

10. A traditional view of Neanderthals is that they lacked the ability to think symbolically. However, recent evidence suggests this view is mistaken. Using an innovative new technique, researchers established that a cave painting in northern Spain was created at least 40,800 years ago. It is therefore likely the painting was made by a Neanderthal.

Which one of the following is an assumption required by the argument?

(A) Neanderthals are known to have possessed the manual dexterity required to create cave paintings like the one in northern Spain.

(B) No species of hominid other than Neanderthals inhabited any part of Europe 40,800 years ago.

(C) The ability to create cave paintings like the one in northern Spain indicates the ability to think symbolically.

(D) The recent evidence regarding the cave painting in northern Spain is the first evidence to suggest that Neanderthals possessed the ability to think symbolically.

(E) Any species of hominid that cannot create cave paintings must lack the ability to think symbolically.

11. To be considered for this year's Gillespie Grant, applications must be received in Gillespie City by October 1. It can take up to ten days for regular mail from Greendale to reach Gillespie City. So if Mary is sending an application by regular mail from Greendale, she will be considered for the grant only if her application is mailed ten days before the due date.

The reasoning in the argument is flawed in that the argument

(A) does not establish that Mary is applying for the Gillespie Grant or mailing anything from Greendale

(B) does not determine how long it takes express mail to reach Gillespie City from Greendale

(C) does not consider the minimum amount of time it takes regular mail from Greendale to reach Gillespie City

(D) presumes, without providing justification, that if Mary's application is received in Gillespie City by October 1, she will satisfy all of the other requirements of the Gillespie Grant application

(E) overlooks the possibility that Mary cannot be certain that her application will arrive in Gillespie City unless she sends it by express mail

12. The Amazon River flows eastward into the Atlantic Ocean from its source in the western part of South America. The land through which the Amazon flows is now cut off from the Pacific Ocean to the west by the Andes Mountains. Yet certain freshwater fish that inhabit the Amazon are descended from now-extinct saltwater fish known to have inhabited the Pacific Ocean but not the Atlantic. For this reason, some scientists hypothesize that the Amazon River once flowed into the Pacific Ocean.

Which one of the following, if true, provides additional evidence in support of the hypothesis that the Amazon River once flowed into the Pacific Ocean?

(A) In many cases, species of freshwater and saltwater fish that share certain characteristics do not in fact share a common ancestor.

(B) Most of the fossilized remains of the now-extinct saltwater fish from the Pacific Ocean date to a period prior to the formation of the Andes Mountains.

(C) Many species of fish that inhabit the Atlantic Ocean are related to fish species that are known to inhabit the Pacific Ocean.

(D) The Andes Mountains extend from the northernmost to the southernmost extremes of the South American continent.

(E) There are very few fish species that are known to be able to survive in both fresh and salt water.

13. Columnist: Banning performance enhancing drugs (PEDs) from sports will not stop their use. They provide too big a competitive advantage. And top athletes will do whatever it takes to gain a big competitive advantage. So PEDs should be allowed, but only if administered under a doctor's care to make sure they are taken only in safe doses. When handled in this fashion the health risks from PEDs disappear.

Which one of the following is an assumption required by the columnist's argument?

(A) Spectators would not lose respect for athletes who they know are taking PEDs.

(B) PEDs would not improve the performance of some athletes more than others.

(C) Athletes do not take PEDs thinking they help performance in cases in which they do not help.

(D) Athletes currently using PEDs cannot find doctors willing to prescribe them.

(E) Using PEDs at unsafe levels does not create a big competitive advantage over using them at safe levels.

GO ON TO THE NEXT PAGE.

14. Max: As evidence mounts showing the terrible changes wrought on the environment by technology, the conclusion that humans must return to a natural way of living becomes irrefutable.

Cora: It is natural for humans to use technology to effect changes on the environment—humans have used technology in that way for many thousands of years. Therefore, your criticism is misguided.

Cora's claim that it is natural for humans to use technology to effect changes on the environment plays which one of the following roles in her response to Max?

(A) It is used to suggest that the alleged cause of terrible changes to the environment cannot be correctly described as unnatural.

(B) It is used to suggest that humans have benefited from many of the changes that they have wrought on the environment.

(C) It is used to suggest that Max's conclusion that technology has wrought terrible changes on the environment has not been supported.

(D) It is used to suggest that the conveniences of modern life will make it difficult for humans to return to a natural way of living.

(E) It is used to suggest that it is a mistake to take the environmental changes caused by technology to be a moral issue.

15. Commentator: The reported epidemic of childhood obesity in our country is a myth. Over the last 8 years, there was only a 1 pound (0.45 kilogram) increase in children's average weight. This is not a substantial increase, so the proportion of children who are obese cannot have increased substantially.

Which one of the following contains flawed reasoning most similar to the flawed reasoning contained in the argument above?

(A) The average summer temperature over the past five years must have increased, since most people believe that summers are getting hotter.

(B) The proportion of employees who earn very high salaries must not have increased more than slightly over the last year, since the average salary has increased only slightly over that time.

(C) The proportion of apartment buildings in the downtown area must have increased substantially in recent years, since a substantial number of office buildings have been converted to apartment buildings during that time.

(D) The average weight of adults must have increased in the last few years, since restaurants have increased the proportion of high-calorie dishes on their menus in recent years.

(E) The average price of a house must be increasing, since the proportion of household income spent on housing has increased over the last eight years.

GO ON TO THE NEXT PAGE.

16. Editorial: The main contention of Kramer's book is that coal companies are to blame for our region's economic difficulties. Kramer bases this contention primarily on allegations made by disgruntled coal company employees that the companies made no significant investments in other industries in our region. Yet the companies invested heavily— albeit sometimes indirectly—in road building and manufacturing in the region. Thus, the book's main contention is simply false.

The reasoning in the editorial's argument is flawed in that this argument

(A) concludes that one party is not to blame for a particular outcome merely on the grounds that another party is to blame for that outcome

(B) concludes that a person's statement is false merely on the grounds that, if accepted as true, it would impugn the reputation of an important industry

(C) rejects an argument merely on the grounds that the person offering the argument has an ulterior motive for doing so

(D) takes a sufficient condition for the coal companies' having made significant investments in other industries in the region to be a necessary condition for their having done so

(E) concludes that a person's statement is false merely on the grounds that an inadequate argument has been given for it

17. Health-care facilities have a duty to protect their patients from unnecessary harm. So, since influenza viruses pose substantial risks to patients, and since vaccines can significantly reduce the spread of these viruses, health-care facilities must institute policies that make influenza vaccinations mandatory for all employees.

Which one of the following is an assumption required by the argument?

(A) Health-care facility employees do not regard mandatory vaccination policies as violating their rights.

(B) Influenza viruses are the most harmful airborne pathogens to which patients risk exposure when entering a health-care facility.

(C) Most patients in health-care facilities are not vaccinated against influenza.

(D) Voluntary vaccination policies at health-care facilities would not adequately protect patients from the risks posed by influenza viruses.

(E) Society has already accepted the idea of mandatory vaccination in other contexts.

18. Etiquette helps people to get along with each other. For example, it prevents people from inadvertently offending one another. While many people criticize etiquette because they believe it has no beneficial effects for society, these same people think that kindness and social harmony are good.

The statements above, if true, most strongly support which one of the following?

(A) Many people who criticize etiquette have contradictory views about etiquette.

(B) Many people have respect for etiquette even though they criticize it.

(C) Many people who criticize etiquette are mistaken about its beneficial effects for society.

(D) If people were more considerate there would be no need for etiquette.

(E) Kindness and social harmony are highly beneficial to society.

19. European wood ants incorporate large quantities of solidified conifer resin into their nests. Conifer resin is a natural disinfectant that has been shown to kill strains of bacteria that can cause disease in wood ants. Thus, the wood ants' use of conifer resin probably came about as a disease-protection measure.

Which one of the following would be most useful to know in order to evaluate the strength of the argument?

(A) whether conifer resin retains its disinfectant properties over very long periods of time

(B) whether the nests of European wood ants generally contain more conifer resin at some times of the year than at others

(C) whether any ant species other than European wood ants use conifer resin in their nests

(D) whether the use of conifer resin affords structural benefits to European wood ants' nests

(E) whether the disinfectant properties of conifer resin evolved as a disease-protection measure for conifer trees

GO ON TO THE NEXT PAGE.

20. Coming up with secure passwords for confidential computer files is difficult. Users prefer passwords that are easy to remember, such as birth dates or relatives' names. Unfortunately, these are the easiest to guess for an outsider who wants to gain access to valuable information. Random configurations of letters and numbers are the hardest to guess, but these are also the easiest for legitimate users to forget. Users who forget their passwords use up the system administrator's time; furthermore, passwords that are very difficult to remember are generally written down by users, and hence pose the greatest security threat of all.

If the statements above are true, which one of the following must also be true?

(A) Computer users should not write down their passwords even if the passwords are hard to remember.
(B) It is expensive to have system administrators constantly resetting forgetful users' passwords.
(C) Passwords that are very easy to guess pose less of a security threat than passwords that are very difficult to remember.
(D) Passwords that are random configurations of letters and numbers are the least likely to result in security breaches.
(E) The easier a password is to remember, the more secure the computer account.

21. If you use a wood stove to heat your home, you should use a wood-pellet stove rather than a regular wood stove. Because wood pellets are made from by-products of manufacturing processes that would otherwise go to landfills, heating a home with a wood-pellet stove will not cause more trees to be felled. The same cannot be said for regular wood stoves. So wood-pellet stoves are better for the environment than are regular wood stoves.

Which one of the following most accurately expresses the overall conclusion drawn in the argument?

(A) Wood pellets are made from waste products of manufacturing processes that would otherwise not be recycled.
(B) Heating a home with a wood-pellet stove is better for the environment than is heating a home with a regular wood stove.
(C) Using a wood-pellet stove to heat one's home does not cause trees to be felled.
(D) Using a regular wood stove to heat one's home causes trees to be felled.
(E) People who use wood stoves to heat their homes should use wood-pellet stoves instead of regular wood stoves.

22. Economist: Gifts of cash or gift cards, which allow the recipient to choose the actual gift, are more highly valued by recipients than are gifts chosen for them by others. In a study, when people were asked how much they would have been willing to pay for gifts chosen for them by others, they responded by citing amounts that were on average only about two-thirds of the actual price of the gifts.

Which one of the following, if true, most seriously weakens the economist's argument?

(A) The rate at which gifts are returned to retailers has been steadily increasing since the rate was first measured.
(B) Gifts of cash and gift cards currently represent only about 14 percent of all gift giving.
(C) People in the study would have been willing to pay more for gifts chosen for them by close friends and relatives than for gifts chosen for them by others.
(D) People are unwilling to sell gifts chosen for them by others unless offered about one and a half times the gift's actual price.
(E) Most retailers require receipts before people can return gifts for refund or exchange.

23. An antitheft device involving an electronic homing beacon has been developed for use in tracking stolen automobiles. Although its presence is undetectable to a car thief and so does not directly deter theft, its use greatly increases the odds of apprehending even the most experienced car thieves. The device is not yet used by a large percentage of car owners, but in cities where only a small percentage of car owners have the device installed, auto thefts have dropped dramatically.

Which one of the following, if true, would most help to explain the dramatic impact of the antitheft device?

(A) Car thieves will tend to be less cautious if they are unaware that a car they have stolen contains a homing beacon.
(B) Typically, the number of cars stolen in cities where the homing beacons are in use was below average before the device was used.
(C) Before the invention of the homing beacon, automobile thieves who stole cars containing antitheft devices were rarely apprehended.
(D) A large proportion of stolen cars are stolen from people who do not live in the cities where they are stolen.
(E) In most cities the majority of car thefts are committed by a few very experienced car thieves.

GO ON TO THE NEXT PAGE.

24. Taken as a whole, the computers that constitute the Internet form a complex, densely interconnected collection that transmits information like the neurons that form the human brain. And like a developing human brain, the Internet is growing at millions of points. So we can expect that the Internet itself will someday gain a humanlike intelligence.

The reasoning in the argument is most vulnerable to criticism on the grounds that it

(A) equates the complexity of an entity with the intelligence of that entity

(B) fails to consider the possibility that other technologies may simulate human intelligence before the Internet does so

(C) draws a dubious analogy between the information that is processed by the human brain and the information that is transmitted on the Internet

(D) fails to give an indication of why the characteristics it focuses on are sufficient for the eventual development of humanlike intelligence

(E) presumes, without providing justification, that the people administering the Internet are interested in developing a system with humanlike intelligence

25. Editorial: Any democratic society is endangered by segmentation into classes of widely differing incomes between which there is little mobility. Such class divisions strengthen divisive political factions that stand in the way of good governance. Since economic expansion gives people more opportunities to improve their economic standing, democratic societies should adopt policies that ensure constant economic expansion.

Which one of the following, if true, would most strengthen the reasoning in the editorial?

(A) Discord within a society tends to increase inequities in the distribution of wealth.

(B) Political factions are sometimes willing to overlook their differences to back policies that are conducive to economic expansion.

(C) Economic expansion results in a proportionally greater increase in earnings for people at low income levels than for people at other income levels.

(D) Economic expansion cannot occur unless there is significant financial investment in the economy by people at the highest income levels.

(E) The presence of divisive political factions can be an obstacle to economic expansion.

S T O P

IF YOU FINISH BEFORE TIME IS CALLED, YOU MAY CHECK YOUR WORK ON THIS SECTION ONLY.
DO NOT WORK ON ANY OTHER SECTION IN THE TEST.

Acknowledgment is made to the following sources from which material has been adapted for use in this test booklet:

David Eagleman, "The Brain on Trial" in *The Atlantic*. ©2011 by The Atlantic Monthly Group.

Michael O'Hear, "What Does the New Brain Science Mean for Criminal Law?" in Life Sentences Blog. ©2011 by Michael O'Hear. http://www.lifesentencesblog.com/?p=2743.

"Physicists Say Big Bang Was 'Nothing Special'" in Space website. ©2012 by TechMediaNetwork.com. http://www.space.com/483-physicists-big-bang-special.html.

Günther Stockinger, "A Peaceable Non-Kingdom." ©1999 by the Stanley Foundation.

Marie Winn, *The Plug-in Drug*. ©1985 by Marie Winn Miller.

Wait for the supervisor's instructions before you open the page to the topic.
Please print and sign your name and write the date in the designated spaces below.
Time: 35 Minutes

General Directions

will have 35 minutes in which to plan and write an essay on the topic inside. Read the topic and the accompanying directions carefully. will probably find it best to spend a few minutes considering the topic and organizing your thoughts before you begin writing. In your essay, sure to develop your ideas fully, leaving time, if possible, to review what you have written. **Do not write on a topic other than the one** **cified. Writing on a topic of your own choice is not acceptable.**

special knowledge is required or expected for this writing exercise. Law schools are interested in the reasoning, clarity, organization, juage usage, and writing mechanics displayed in your essay. How well you write is more important than how much you write.

nfine your essay to the blocked, lined area on the front and back of the separate Writing Sample Response Sheet. Only that area will be roduced for law schools. Be sure that your writing is legible.

Both this topic sheet and your response sheet must be turned in to the testing staff before you leave the room.

Topic Code	Print Your Full Name Here		
156059	Last	First	M.I.

Date	Sign Your Name Here
/ /	

LSAC®

Scratch Paper
Do not write your essay in this space.

LSAT® Writing Sample Topic

> <u>Directions</u>: The scenario presented below describes two choices, either one of which can be supported on the basis of the information given. Your essay should consider both choices and argue for one over the other, based on the two specified criteria and the facts provided. There is no "right" or "wrong" choice: a reasonable argument can be made for either.

The astronomy department at a university is building an observatory. It will build either a visible-spectrum observatory, which uses an optical telescope, or a radio observatory, which uses a telescope built to detect radio waves from space. Using the facts below, write an essay in which you argue for building one type of observatory over the other based on the following two criteria:

- The observatory should be useful for productive scholarly research conducted by the department's faculty that will contribute to the field.
- The observatory should be useful as an educational tool.

Most faculty members in the department do work that could make use of a visible-spectrum observatory for research projects. These faculty collectively publish a large number of research papers. There are a large number of visible-spectrum observatories around the world being used for scholarly research. A visible-spectrum observatory could be used as part of most astronomy classes. Many graduate students in the department work in areas that would not make use of a visible-spectrum observatory.

It is relatively easy for researchers at radio observatories to collaborate with other radio observatories to conduct large, groundbreaking projects. Such projects can monopolize the use of an observatory for extended periods of time. One of the university's most famous faculty members specializes in radio astronomy. Many graduate students in the department came to the university to study with this professor. Few other faculty members would use the observatory for their research. A radio observatory could attract new faculty members who use radio telescopes in their research. A new radio observatory would be difficult to integrate into the astronomy classes of most students. WPAB15

Scratch Paper
Do not write your essay in this space.

Writing Sample Response Sheet

DO NOT WRITE
IN THIS SPACE

Begin your essay in the lined area below.
Continue on the back if you need more space.

COMPUTING YOUR SCORE

Directions:

1. Use the Answer Key on the next page to check your answers.

2. Use the Scoring Worksheet below to compute your raw score.

3. Use the Score Conversion Chart to convert your raw score into the 120–180 scale.

Scoring Worksheet

1. Enter the number of questions you answered correctly in each section.

	Number Correct
SECTION I..................	_____
SECTION II.................	_____
SECTION III...............	_____
SECTION IV	_____

2. Enter the sum here: _____

This is your Raw Score.

Conversion Chart
For Converting Raw Score to the 120–180 LSAT Scaled Score
LSAT Form 8LSN132

Reported Score	Raw Score Lowest	Raw Score Highest
180	98	99
179	97	97
178	96	96
177	95	95
176	*	*
175	94	94
174	93	93
173	92	92
172	91	91
171	90	90
170	89	89
169	88	88
168	86	87
167	85	85
166	83	84
165	82	82
164	80	81
163	79	79
162	77	78
161	75	76
160	73	74
159	71	72
158	70	70
157	68	69
156	66	67
155	64	65
154	62	63
153	60	61
152	59	59
151	57	58
150	55	56
149	53	54
148	52	52
147	50	51
146	48	49
145	46	47
144	45	45
143	43	44
142	41	42
141	40	40
140	38	39
139	37	37
138	35	36
137	34	34
136	33	33
135	31	32
134	30	30
133	29	29
132	28	28
131	27	27
130	26	26
129	25	25
128	24	24
127	23	23
126	22	22
125	21	21
124	20	20
123	19	19
122	18	18
121	*	*
120	0	17

*There is no raw score that will produce this scaled score for this form.

ANSWER KEY

SECTION I

1.	E	8.	D	15.	A	22.	D
2.	D	9.	C	16.	B	23.	D
3.	B	10.	E	17.	E	24.	E
4.	A	11.	C	18.	B	25.	A
5.	A	12.	B	19.	D		
6.	D	13.	C	20.	B		
7.	C	14.	B	21.	B		

SECTION II

1.	B	8.	C	15.	D	22.	D
2.	C	9.	A	16.	C	23.	E
3.	A	10.	C	17.	D		
4.	E	11.	D	18.	D		
5.	A	12.	E	19.	A		
6.	A	13.	B	20.	C		
7.	D	14.	E	21.	E		

SECTION III

1.	A	8.	D	15.	A	22.	D
2.	C	9.	B	16.	D	23.	C
3.	E	10.	A	17.	B	24.	D
4.	B	11.	D	18.	E	25.	E
5.	C	12.	E	19.	E	26.	C
6.	B	13.	C	20.	A		
7.	E	14.	D	21.	B		

SECTION IV

1.	B	8.	A	15.	B	22.	D
2.	E	9.	E	16.	E	23.	E
3.	D	10.	C	17.	D	24.	D
4.	E	11.	C	18.	C	25.	C
5.	B	12.	B	19.	D		
6.	A	13.	E	20.	C		
7.	B	14.	A	21.	E		

LSAT® PREP TOOLS

The Official LSAT SuperPrep II™

SuperPrep II contains everything you need to prepare for the LSAT—a guide to all three LSAT question types, three actual LSATs, explanations for all questions in the three practice tests, answer keys, writing samples, and score-conversion tables, plus invaluable test-taking instructions to help with pacing and timing. SuperPrep has long been our most comprehensive LSAT preparation book, and SuperPrep II is even better. The practice tests in SuperPrep II are PrepTest 62 (December 2010 LSAT), PrepTest 63 (June 2011 LSAT), and one test that has never before been disclosed.

With this book you can

• Practice on genuine LSAT questions

• Review explanations for right and wrong answers

• Target specific categories for intensive review

• Simulate actual LSAT conditions

LSAC sets the standard for LSAT prep—and SuperPrep II raises the bar!

Available at your favorite bookseller.

LSAC.org

Law School Admission Council